STATE AND MAIN
a screenplay

David Mamet has written twenty-three plays, eight
collections of essays, two novels, five children's books, two
books of poetry, and eighteen films, including *The Verdict*
and *Wag the Dog* for which he received Academy Award
nominations. *State and Main* is his seventh feature as a
writer-director, after *House of Games, Things Change,
Homicide, Oleanna, The Spanish Prisoner,* and *The Winslow
Boy*. Mamet has received numerous awards, including the
Pulitzer Prize in 1984 for *Glengarry Glen Ross*.

STATE AND MAIN

a screenplay by
David Mamet

Methuen

A METHUEN SCREENPLAY

10 9 8 7 6 5 4 3 2 1

Published in 2001 by Methuen Publishing Ltd
215 Vauxhall Bridge Rd, London SW1V 1EJ

First published in the United States by Newmarket Press.

Methuen Publishing Limited Reg. No. 3543167

A CIP catalogue record for this book is available from the British Library

ISBN 0 413 76510 5

Typeset by SX Composing DTP, Rayleigh, Essex
Printed and bound in Great Britain by Cox and Wyman Ltd, Reading, Berkshire

INTRODUCTION

by David Mamet

The old film story has a crew shooting a car commercial on top of a mountain. It is the 'magic hour' shot, which is to say, sunset. The shot is set up when the location manager says, 'This spot is good, but the spot one hundred yards away is superb.'

Everyone schlepps over, and there, on a promontory, is the most magnificent view in the world – the valley stretches away below, all is perfect save the one pine tree occupying the only space to put the product. They chop down the tree, put the car there, get the shot, and repair to the local airport.

Everyone is having a drink, waiting for the plane, and the bartender says, 'You folks look happy.'

'Happy,' the director says, 'Of course we're happy. We just shot at the most beautiful vista I have ever seen.'

'Oh,' says the bartender, 'You must have been up on Lone Pine Ridge.'

Priceless film lore. Van humor.

Most films are made on location, and location shooting means hundreds of hours in the van. We pile into the van to scout locations, to revisit chosen locations with the Art Department, to revisit with the Director of Photography and the Storyboard Artist, to revisit with Locations, Stunts, Effects. . . Four hours a day times five days a week times ten weeks of preproduction is two hundred hours in the van; we talk on the cell phone, and gossip and exchange film stories. Getting dishy or silly is an effective strategy to take the edge off The Van – in which locale it never gets more 'entre nous'.

The most prized stories, of course, are the morbid: who threw up on camera, who got on the wrong plane and went to Thailand, who forgot to remove his or her body mike, and repaired to the camper to make love with an unauthorized person (while the sound man, of course, put it out over the PA).

This week my favorite is the couple who leased their house for a shoot. ('We'll leave it better than we found it' – a phrase, in itself, capable of raising a chuckle in the van. Other van howlers: 'It plays in one [shot],' 'I see one bare lightbulb,' 'Don't worry.') One gag involved the couple's house catching fire. The technicians built a false front on the house and, on the day, set it aflame. The gag went awry and the whole house went up in flames. The owners, standing on a neighbor's lawn, looked at the marvelously believable effect and clapped. 'They clapped three times,' the eyewitness said.

Now, we were shooting in a late Victorian house. The owner had grown up there. Her grandfather built it, after the Civil War. 'Touch anything,' she said, 'except the wallpaper.' It was original to the house, flocked and multicolored, irreplaceable, historically significant, and so on. And we were So Careful, until the last minute of the last day of night shooting, and the sun was coming up, and we had to get it and get out.

'I need an eyeline,' the star said. So someone took two long pieces of fluorescent tape, and spread them in an X behind the camera, which is to say, on the wallpaper. When I punched out to go home, the camera crew was wrapping out, and our scene painter was on a ladder, a small Maglite in his teeth, three brushes in his hand, endeavoring to patch the ruined High Victorian Wallpaper. Well, we didn't leave it better than we found it, but we sure left it different.

Q: What director of a cowboy movie found a great location in a Western state, and then informed the studio that a forty-acre plain would have to have an underground irrigation system installed? (He wanted the location for a huge set-piece gun battle on horses.)

'Why,' they said, 'it's green now.'

'But what,' he said, 'if I have to do more than one take?'

The studio, chastened, nodded and approved the expenditure – not realizing that, after the first take, the pasture would, of course, be mud; and, ignorant, into the bargain, that the fortuitously found location belonged, that's right, to the director.

Van dish: What suicide was not a suicide, what marriage not a marriage; who 'fixed' the Oscars, who poisoned his wife, who was a bit too kind to animals; and updates on the various run-of-the-mill dope fiends, lushes, psychoneurotics, and paedophiles who populate this business that we've chosen.

One feels, and this is much of the joy, that it's always been the same – the stories are the same, the names change: strike out those libel laws prohibit mentioning, fill in Roman Navarro, Wallace Reid, Roscoe Arbuckle, Mary Miles Minter, William Desmond, Marilyn Monroe.

Great story: from Jack Lemmon - *Some Like It Hot*, first day, Billy Wilder comes to Jack and Tony Curtis and says, 'Boys: be good all the time, 'cause when the broad's good, we're gonna print it.'

Another Billy Wilder story: Paramount comes to him, on *Stalag 17*.

'It's gonna be a big hit foreign,' they say. 'We don't want to hurt the German market. How about, if instead of being German, the camp guards were Poles. What do you think...?'

'I would,' says Wilder, 'but most of my family died at Dachau.'

Hollywood wisdom has it that one can't make a movie about

Hollywood. Per contra, however, *Sullivan's Travels*, *What Price Hollywood* (remade, of course, as *A Star Is Born*), *The Bad and the Beautiful*, etc. – in fact, one might apply the maxim 'In time of peace prepare for war, in time of war. . .' and translate the Received Wisdom: 'About time for another movie about Hollywood.'

My attempt is the film *State and Main*. It was inspired by the Lone Pine Ridge story. This time around, a film company, three days away from principal photography, has lost its location. (A small town, out of which they were kicked when the movie's star was discovered in flagrante with a minor.)

The film company descends on a new town and proceeds, in those three days, of course, to 'leave it better than they found it.'

I am currently in preproduction for another film, and spending eons in the Van in and around Montreal.

'Yes,' we say, 'you can shoot Montreal for anywhere. You can shoot it for Boston, you can go around a corner and shoot it for eighteenth-century Paris – you can shoot it for New York. . . .'

And, at the end of the day, the van convulses itself with speculation about Location Scouting three hundred years hence: 'Pluto,' they would say. 'Man, I love Pluto—you can shoot it for Jupiter, you can shoot it for the Moon, parts of it look like the Asteroids . . .'

Van humor.

STILLS

(*left to right*) Philip Seymour Hoffman, David Paymer, Alec Baldwin, Sarah Jessica Parker, and William H. Macy

Top: (left to right) Julia Stiles, William H. Macy and Linda Kimbrough

Bottom: Sarah Jessica Parker and Alec Baldwin

Top: Rebecca Pidgeon and Philip Seymour Hoffman

Bottom: Lonnie Smith and William H. Macy

Top: Alec Baldwin

Bottom: Philip Seymour Hoffman

Top: Rebecca Pidgeon

Bottom: Julia Stiles

Top: Director David Mamet and Alec Baldwin

Bottom: William H. Macy and Philip Seymour Hoffman

Top: Philip Seymour Hoffman and Rebecca Pidgeon

Bottom: Clark Gregg, Alec Baldwin, Robert Walsh, and David Paymer

Top: Patti LuPone and Charles Durning

Bottom: Julia Stiles and Rebecca Pidgeon

STATE AND MAIN

CAST

FADE IN:

EXT. FIREHOUSE. DAY.
ANN *is walking down the street. The firedog runs out of the firehouse. She gives the dog a biscuit, and pats him on the head.*
The FIREMAN *is out front with a cup of coffee.* ANN *hands him a poster.*

EXT. STATE AND MAIN – INTERSECTION. DAY.
MORRIS *and* SPUD, *two codgers, are about to cross the street when they hear a beeping and stop. As they cross, we see the tail end of a van, and the group nods in that direction.*

MORRIS: You hear that?
SPUD: Yes, I hear it.
MORRIS: Drive a man to drink. Took me near half an hour, get across the street yesterday.
SPUD: I saw Budgie Gagnon, leaning on the bank of the building. Said, 'What are you doin'?' He said, 'I'm waitin' for the 'leven o'clock crossing . . .

As MORRIS *and* SPUD *speak a car is coming down the street, and bounces in the pothole.*

MORRIS: Ywanna fix something, you should fix the *pothole.* Yessir, they should be trussed up, thrown off some high building

DOUG MACKENZIE, *a young Republican type, walks up to join them.*

DOUG: Who's that?

3

MORRIS: Whoever spent ten, f'teen thousand dollars, a new
    traffic light, you could grow old, paint your house before
    it lets you cross the street, and *then*, not fix the pothole.
SPUD: What was wrong with the old traffic light?

INT. COFFEE CORNER – DAY
They enter the Coffee Corner. CARLA, *the nubile waitress, is
serving the folk, and* JACK, *the owner, is behind the counter.*

DOUG: I'm glad you asked . . . I'll *tell* you what was wrong
    with it. And what was wrong with it was it was behind
    the times. Now: You want to bring *business* into this
    town? You have to plan for a Waterford that Does Not
    Exist. Not at this moment, *no* . . .
ANN: Morning, darling.
DOUG: Morning.
CARLA: Hi, Annie.

ANN *hands* CARLA *a poster.*

ANN: Morning, Carla.

DOUG *and the two codgers move to a table by the window where*
CARLA *brings them coffee.* ANN *talks to a woman at the counter*
(MAUDE).

MORRIS: . . . the damn thing . . .
SPUD: No, I'm serious, election's coming up, a lot of people
    are pretty upset . . .
DOUG: They are . . . Yes. I'm *sure* they are . . .
MAUDE: Annie, I'm going to be a lil late for the rehearsal,
    tonight.
ANN: S'okay Maude. You know your lines . . . ?

4

DOUG: . . . I'm sure that people are upset . . .

MAUDE: I know 'em, I don't know what order they come in . . .

ANN: We'll work it out . . .

JACK: What're they on about?

ANN: Traffic light.

JACK: Waal, no, th' traffic light's Doug's thing. That's his thing, fine.

DOUG: *Thank* you, Jack, and –

JACK: But we got to talk about the pothole.

DOUG: *Jack* . . .

JACK: A public office is a public trust . . . This is why this is America. Question is: who owns the street.

Outside the front booth, on the street, the airport van cruises by.

EXT. STATE AND MAIN – DAY.
As they walk out we hear a high pitched beeping sound at the traffic light. We see DOC WILSON *crossing the street, holding his doctor's bag. An* ELDERLY MAN *approaches* DOC *at the crossing. As* WALT *and* BILL *walk, the airport van follows them.*

ELDERLY MAN: Doc, those pills, y'gave me for my back? I'm not sure that they work.

DOC WILSON: Well, I'm not sure *either*, but y'don't hear *me* complain . . . come by th'office, end of th'afternoon.

ELDERLY MAN: Thanks Doc . . .

BILL: *This* is your movie, this is small town America.

WALT: Town in New Hampshire was small town America too. Forty thousand dollars a day, to shoot on the street. And *then* they kicked us out . . .

They stop in front of a rack of fifty 'factory seconds'. Black and

*red hunting jackets, in front of the sporting goods store. The sign
reads* 'FACTORY SECONDS, FIVE DOLLARS'.

BILL: A jacket for five dollars . . . I can buy this town for fifty
    bucks.

WALT: You told me that about the *last* town.

BILL: Yeah, but they never made a movie here.

WALT: I'm bleeding, Bill, I'm *bleeding* . . .

BILL: . . . why am I here . . . ?

WALT: What, what, what, what do they got, that can pass for
    The Old Mill . . .

BILL *shows* WALT *a brochure from Waterford, which shows a
picture of the Old Mill.* WALT *reads.*

WALT: 'The Waterford Mill, built in 1825, and long a tourist
    attraction . . . ' Wake up Uberto.

Angle. The airport van. UBERTO *is asleep.* BILL *wakes him up.*

UBERTO: Where are we?

WALT: Givvem a cigarette . . .

UBERTO *comes out of the car and squints around.*

UBERTO: . . . they ship our Old Mill from New Hampshire . . .?

BILL: They're holding our Old Mill for ransom.

UBERTO: We build it?

BILL: We don't have to build it.

BILL *shows* UBERTO *the brochure.*

UBERTO: We build the firehut . . . ?

6

WALT *shows* UBERTO *the firehouse.* UBERTO *looks through viewfinder.*

UBERTO: We have to lose the window.
WALT: . . . we can't lose the wind . . .
UBERTO (*pulling out storyboards*): Then I can't do this shot
. . . you wants me to push in – I can't push in through
the window . . . We go back to New Hampshire?
BILL: NO, we can't ever go back to New Hampshire.

A pickup truck with two calves in it stops. The driver seen from the back is a farmer smoking a pipe.

WALT: NO, we're gonna stay here. This is what my people
died for. The right to make a movie in this town.

INT. TAVERN INN LOBBY. DAY.
A desk CLERK *looks up. Behind the desk a display of several souvenir plates, 'Souvenir of Waterford, VT', with a picture of the Old Mill on them.* WALT *picks one up and hands it to* BILL.

CLERK: May I help you?
WALT (*followed Bill*): I want to talk to the manager . . .

WALT *talks into his cell phone as he talks to the* CLERK.

CLERK: Would you like a room?
BILL: Na, we wanna rent the whole hotel.
WALT (*into phone*): Hello, Tracy; we gotta new town. We're
. . . where are we?

Beat. BILL *looks around, sees a sign on the desk. Consults his tourist folder. As they talk they walk into the deserted ballroom*

7

and play shuffleboard and archery.

BILL (*carrying Waterford plate*): Waterford, Vermont.
WALT: . . . you got to get me that street for nothing . . .
BILL: I will.
WALT (*into phone*): Waterford, Vermont. Where is it? *That's*
    where it is . . .

WALT *carries the shuffleboard stick over his shoulder.*

INT. WALT'S OFFICE. NIGHT.
WALT *is talking on a cellphone. A male* PRODUCTION
ASSISTANT *is bringing in bags of equipment.* BILL *is still sitting
perched on a desk, typing into his computer.* UBERTO *is sitting on
a couch smoking. We see the shuffleboard stick on the desk, and
the Old Mill plate on the wall.*

WALT (*to phone*): Because, because . . . we don't *have* to build
    an Old Mill – they *have* an Old Mill – *yeah.* It's on a
    stream – that's where you *put* a mill.
BILL: . . . they run on water.
WALT (*to phone*): Now: I'm looking at the . . .

WALT *gestures for* BILL *who hands him the storyboards.*

WALT: I've got scene *twelve* . . . (*to* CARLA) Shouldn't you be
    in school . . . ?
CARLA: It's night.
WALT (*to phone as he shows the Old Mill storyboards to camera*)
    Scene *twelve* . . . arrival at the mill.

Angle: CLERK *enters.*

CLERK Mr Price, Mr Price . . . ? (*he hands* WALT *flowers*)
BILL: What . . . ?

They go back to the flowers. WALT *takes the card, reads.*

WALT: 'Bring it in on time and there's more where these
    came from. Marty. PS I want to talk to you about a
    product tie-in . . . '
CLERK: I'll put the, in your r . . .
WALT: Somebody make a note. I want li . . . , for the broad
    . . . what does she like? Lilacs. Okay. A truck of lilacs
    when the broad comes. And get something for Bob
    Barrenger, get him, what does he like . . . ?
CLERK: Bob Barrenger . . . Bob . . . Bob Barrenger's in this
    movie . . . ?
WALT: That's cor . . .
CLERK: (*awed*) He's staying here? Bob Barrenger is staying
    he . . . ?
WALT: Put something in his room. What does he like?
BILL: Fourteen-year-old girls.
WALT: Well, get him something else and let's get out of here
    in one piece. Get him a half of a 28-year-old girl.

INT. PRODUCTION OFFICE – WAITING ROOM. DAY.
Insert: Front page: Burlington Banner. *Picture of movie star Bob
Barrenger, and banner headline: 'Waterford chosen as site of new
Bob Barrenger film. A story of small town life based on . . . '*
CARLA *knocks on the door to the back room. Voices from inside.
Outside, on two chairs, the* MAYOR, *George Bailey, a man in his
fifties, and* JOE WHITE, *the writer, dressed in an army field jacket
and jeans, waiting to be admitted.*
JOE *is reading an old 'Welcome to Waterford' tourist folder. The
door to the room opens, and* JOE *stands, looks inside, squints.*

Takes off his reading glasses, and puts on another pair.

JOE (*to the open door*): I, I'm sorr . . . (*as the door closes, to a
      passing aide*) . . . I lost my *typewriter* . . .

CARLA *brushes past them.*

CARLA: Hi, Mr Bailey . . .
MAYOR: Carla, would you tell them that I'm . . .
WALT (*from inside*): . . . What? What is it?

CARLA *enters the back room. As she does so, she passes the* FIRST
ASSISTANT DIRECTOR, *who is on the telephone.*

FIRST A D: Could I speak to my wife, please – ?

Camera takes us with CARLA *into the back room. Past the* FIRST
ASSISTANT DIRECTOR.

SECRETARY: (*to* FIRST A D) You've got a call . . .

INT. PRODUCTION OFFICE & WALT'S OFFICE. DAY.
*Inside the room, production boards being carried in, blackboards,
schedules taped to the wall, sketches of Main Street, a large 'days
till shoot . . . 4' sign. The Old Mill plate is on the desk.
The* PRODUCTION DESIGNER *is bent over a worktable. He holds
a compass, and refers to blueprints and a scale model of the
firehouse and the Old Mill, which are on the table.*
WALT *is holding glossy photographs, and leafs through them as the*
PRODUCTION DESIGNER *talks. They leaf through storyboards.
We see that* WALT *is leafing through glossy photos of horses.*
WALT *has the shuffleboard stick over his shoulder.*
Angle on storyboards of firehouse scene.

PRODUCTION DESIGNER: And Uberto tells me he can't take this shot, unless they let me take out the firehouse window.

COSTUME DESIGNER: Walt, I've got to talk to you about her nude scene.

CARLA *enters*.

WALT: Aren't you ever in school?
CARLA: There's other things to be learned.
WALT: Izzat so?
CARLA: The Mayor's outside.
WALT: What's his name?
CARLA: Mr Bailey.

WALT *goes to the door, opens it, looks around.*

EXT. WALT'S OFFICE. DAY
JOE *reading the* Burlington Banner. *He stands up.*

WALT: Mr Bailey . . . Mr Bailey . . . ?

WALT *and the* MAYOR *enter Walt's office.*

JOE (*to passing secretary*) I lost my *typewriter* . . . ?
FIRST A D: (*passing*) Yes, could I please speak to my *wife* . . . ?

Angle: interior Walt's office.

WALT: I have to tell you, I can not *express* to you how *happy* . . .
MAYOR: And we're glad to have you here . . .
WALT: My golly, you know? All my life I grew up in the city,

11

but every summer . . . would you like a cigar?

MAYOR: (*of cigars*) Aren't these *illegal?*

WALT: Why would they be illegal?

BILL: . . . there's a trade embargo against Cuba.

Pause.

MAYOR: Well, you know, Walt, I just wanted to say that anything I could do.

WALT: That's very kind of . . . as a matter of fact, one, I hate to *bother* you with . . .

MAYOR: . . . not at all . . .

WALT: . . . we need the shooting permit for Main Street . . .

MAYOR: *Whatever* you need. The City Council, of course, has to pass on your . . .

WALT: . . . the city council . . .

MAYOR: On your 'permit', but that is less than a formality.

WALT: . . . it is?

MAYOR: I *am* the City Council. We meet Friday, and I . . .

WALT: George, that is so kind of you.

MAYOR: And, my *wife* wanted to, wanted me to ask you, we'd like to *welcome* you, we'd, she'd like to have you to dinner at our house. (*beat*) I don't mean to be . . .

He hands an invitation to WALT.

WALT: Are you kidding me? We would be de . . .

Phone rings.
WALT *motions to an aide, who writes in green on a production board: Tuesday 12th, dinner, Mayor.*

MAYOR: Well, I won't take more of your time . . .

BILL: Walt, it's Marty on the coast . . .

MAYOR: We'll see you Tuesday, then . . .

WALT *starts for the phone.*

WALT: It's one of the great, great pleasures meeting you . . .

MAYOR *leaves the office.*

BILL: It's Marty on the coast –
WALT On the coast? Of *course* he's on the coast, where's he
    gonna be, the *Hague* . . .

WALT *goes to the phone.*

WALT (*into phone*) What? *Marty!* Hi. We're . . . (*Pause*) The
    new town is cheaper than the other town. We're going to
    save a *for* . . . because . . . because we don't *have* to
    rebuild the Old Mill, they've got an Old Mill . . . they've
    got a firehouse . . . they . . .

A PRODUCTION ASSISTANT *comes in, installing a piece of*
equipment. She brushes past the drywipe board, where we see she
wipes out 'Dinner, Mayor'.

WALT: Baby, baby, I want to save the money just as much as
    you do . . . no, no it's not coming out of my pocket, it's
    going *into* my pock . . . my . . . my and *your* pock . . .
    yeah? Okay. A product placement – tell me ab . . . he's
    going through a tunnel. (*to* PRODUCTION ASSISTANT)
    Whoa, whoa, whoa . . . you wiped out the board.
    DINNER WITH THE MAYOR, TUESDAY NIGHT, write it in
    red. That's all we need, to miss dinner with . . .

FIRST ASSISTANT DIRECTOR *sticks his head into the room.*

FIRST A D: We can't shoot in the Old Mill.
WALT (*to phone*): Wait a sec, Marty. Call us back. Two
    minutes.

He hangs up. Pause.

FIRST A D: We can't shoot in the Old Mill.
WALT: I just saw the Mayor, he said anything we . . .
FIRST A D: It burnt down.
BILL: When did it burn down?

FIRST ASSISTANT DIRECTOR *takes out a book,* The History of
    Waterford, *and reads.*

FIRST A D: 1960. 'Part of a spate of suspicious fires, the Old
    Mill, the . . . '

*He hands polaroids of the burnt Old Mill around. All look at
them.*
Angle insert: Debris by some water.

WALT: You told me they had an Old Mill here...
FIRST A D: '. . . suspicions of arson, these fires, believed set
    by a disturbed teenager, were, in fact, the inspiration for
    the formation of . . . '

He puts the Polaroids down by the model of the Old Mill.
Beat.
JOE *enters.*

BILL: But, does it have to be an Old Mill?
JOE: Hi.
WALT: Does it have to be an Old Mill? Where have you
    been?

14

JOE: I was in New Hampshire. I was at the Old Location.

WALT: We can't shoot the Old Mill.

JOE (*laughs*): You know, they told me there were gonna be some jokes. Kid the New Guy . . .

BILL: The Mill burnt down.

He shows the Polaroids – they show the debris, and Bill standing by them.

BILL: *Wonderful* scr . . .

JOE (*pause*): Can't . . . can't you build the Old Mill?

WALT: We're out of money.

JOE: You built an Old Mill in New Hampshire . . .

BILL: They're holding it for ransom.

JOE: Uh – why did we have to leave New Hampshire?

Pause. The phone rings.

WALT: Hallo? *Marty*? (*to* JOE) What would they have used instead of an old mill? We need it tonight. (*to phone*) Marty? Yeah you were saying . . . ?

JOE: I can't write it. I lost my typewriter.

WALT: Grace: get Mr White a typewriter.

JOE: I can only write on a manual.

WALT: I know the feeling.

JOE: Well, you know, you know, that's a lie, I, I . . .

WALT: Grace . . .

JOE: That's a real *fault*, I . . .

WALT: Grace. Get Mr White a manual typewriter. (*to* JOE) It's not a lie, it's a gift for fiction. And somebody find me my lucky pillow.

He nods at JOE, *who leaves the office. Hold on* WALT *as he looks at horse pictures.*

WALT: How big is this horse?

BILL (*looking at the resume*): Fifteen hands.

WALT: What is that in fingers . . . ? Just kidding, get me this horse.

BILL: This horse is booked.

WALT: Tell the guy, get me the horse, I'll give him an Associate Producer credit.

Angle on JOE, *outside Walt's door, looking at his script and shaking his head.*
Angle: his POV.
Insert: the script. We see for the first time that the name of the script is 'The Old Mill', *by Joseph Turner White.*
We hear raucous laughter from WALT, *et al, in the BG.*

INT. TAVERN INN LOBBY. DAY.

JOE *passes the* FIRST ASSISTANT DIRECTOR *on the telephone, sees* BILL. *The* PRODUCTION ASSISTANTS *are heaping mounds of luggage.*

FIRST A D: Well, no, the labor with a first child can sometimes be prolonged, as much as . . .

BILL (*to* PRODUCTION ASSISTANT): Find Walt's lucky pillow.

JOE: What's an Associate Producer credit?

BILL: It's what you give to your secretary instead of a raise.

The CLERK *in an argument with an* ELECTRICIAN.

ELECTRICIAN: . . . put a VHS and an air-conditioner and a refrigerator in that room, she's going to blow . . .

A DELIVERY MAN *appears with an invoice and a crate.* CLERK *checks the invoice against a list.*

16

CLERK: This isn't Evian water.

DELIVERY MAN: It's *water*.

CLERK: I can't sign for it, I'm . . .

ELECTRICIAN: . . . she's going to blow.

CLERK: Well, you re-wire . . .

ELECTRICIAN: I rewire it, I'm going to have to tear out half, the, look, what do they need with fifty-four telephone lines?

CLERK: Freddy, Freddy, I *work* for these people, you . . . it *is* to be done, you see *that* it's done . . .

The GIRL PRODUCTION ASSISTANT *arrives with a huge bouquet.*

GIRL P A: I found lilacs!

CLERK: *Wonderful,* that's . . .

JOE *enters, goes up to the desk.*

JOE: Did they find . . .

The CLERK's *eyes turn toward the door. Everyone's eyes turn towards the door.*

JOE (*as he writes in his notebook*): Did they find my typewriter . . .

Angle, his POV. BOB BARRENGER, *the star, screamingly fit, leather jacket, jeans, carrying a gym bag. He smiles, goes up to the desk. As he goes up to the desk, teenagers, who have been waiting in the lobby, crowd to him.*

CLERK: I told you!!! All of you get back!!! Get back!!! This man is a *guest* here . . . !!!

17

The teenagers retreat.

BOB: Hello, I'm . . .

CLERK: Oh, Sir, I know who you are . . .

BOB: Bob Barrenger, I'm with the mo . . .

CLERK: Sir, sir, we're so, we're . . . (*he hits the bell*) Front!
Front! We are so, I've seen, I know everybody *says* this,
but I've seen *every every* one of your . . . (*to*
ELECTRICIAN) Freddy, take Mr . . .

ELECTRICIAN: . . . I'm working.

CLERK: Your room is 414 through seventeen. I'm Scott
Larkin. *Anything* you need, this is my private . . . (*hands
him his card*)

BOB: Glad to meet you Scottie. I'm just here to do a job, just
like the rest of these . . .

FIRST ASSISTANT DIRECTOR *walks through the lobby.*

FIRST A D (*to* JOE): Have you got the new pages on the Old
Mill? Hey, Bob.

BOB: Hey, Tommy. Heard your wife's having a baby.

FIRST A D: That's right.

BOB: Do you know who the *father* is . . . ?

FIRST A D: They think it's your First Wife . . .

BOB: That Could Be.

An old man, the BELLHOP, *is sitting by the front door, eating his
lunch out of an old galvanized tin lunch bucket. He puts it down,
and gets up and takes the bags.*
The lobby is filled with gawkers. CHUCKIE, *a young boy holding
a bat and ball, comes over with an autograph pad.*

FIRST A D: (*to* CLERK) I'm going to give you a list of Mr
Barrenger's dietary requirements.

18

CHUCKIE: Mr Barrenger, I . . .

CLERK: Not today, not today, Chuckie, Mr. Barrenger has just . . .

BOB *brushes him aside.*

BOB (*to* CHUCKIE): How do you spell that, son? With an IE? Chuck? What're your *hobbies* . . . ?

CHUCKIE: Baseball.

BOB: Baseball! That's the national sport! Gimme that!

He takes Chuckie's ball and autographs it, 'CHUCKIE! From your pal, Bob Barrenger.'

BOB: Chuckie . . .

Camera pans off BOB, *as he talks to* CHUCKIE, *and on to* JOE, *who is wandering around the lobby.*
The FIRST ASSISTANT DIRECTOR *comes up to* JOE.

FIRST A D: How you doin' with the Old Mill pages?

JOE: I need my typewriter. Did they find my . . . ?

INT. COFFEE CORNER. DAY.
Angle insert. Pan off 'Trials of the Heart' *theatrical poster.*
MORRIS, SPUD *and* JACK *sitting in the same window booth chatting. Phone rings.* CARLA *answers it.*

CARLA: Coffee Corner.

JACK: Fellow gets a calf, it's forty below, calf gets out, he *hears* that animal, he's going to, get up, pull on his jeans . . .

The MAYOR *is taking a pack of Camels from* JACK.
Angle on CARLA, *at the counter, reading the script of 'The Old Mill' surreptitiously.*

MORRIS: He's going to *get* that calf.

SPUD: Mmm . . .

CARLA (*into phone*): Thank you. (*hangs up; to* JACK *who is behind the grill*) Vanilla Frappe. Two tuna BLTs . . .

JACK: What's a Tuna BLT?

CARLA: Oh, *Dad* . . . didn't you read in *People Magazine* . . .

ANN: Well, I for one, am glad of a little diversion and I'm glad they're here . . .

DOUG: What I am *saying*, is, we have to Look Out For Our Own . . . Now: they want to close down Main Street . . .

JACK: Y'wanna talk about Main Street, whyn't cha fix the *pothole*?

ANN: Doug, it's, what did you . . . ? Three days, three, four days. We'll have a record of our wonderful life.

DOUG: Annie: you stick to the Amateur Theatricals. This isn't quite the same thing, you see? This is Big Business, in *which*, our Life (*to* MAYOR) s'no less a *commodity* than . . . than our . . .

ANN: Water or mineral deposits.

DOUG: Waal, that's what I'm saying.

JACK: Communist country, he hears that *Calf*, it's two a.m., four feet of snow, what does he say? 'That's the State's Calf out there . . . ' He rolls over. "Wake me at Ten.'

CARLA, *who has been waiting for the order to be prepared, takes it from her father, starts out the door.*

CARLA: I think that they're nice.

ANN: I'm sure they are.

JACK: That's the difference, Communism and . . . *you*

20

know . . .

SPUD: Communism's over.

JACK: That's what they said about Warner Brothers, 1985,
   but if you look at their price-per-*share* . . .

CARLA: Dad, I've got to go to Terry's house to study
   tonight . . .

JACK: I want you home by Nine.

DOUG: I want to tell you something, Ann: you stay *soft* all
   your life, people *despise* you; it awakens Avarice in them,
   they take advantage of you, and that's Human Nature.

ANN *gets up. She starts to exit the Coffee Corner.* JACK *picks up
a copy of* People *magazine.*

*Insert: An article on Bob Barrenger. Carla has gone over it with a
highlighter. The article is called 'Bob Barrenger's Little Problem'.
Angle: Interior Coffee Corner.*

DOUG: We on for tomorrow night?

ANN: After Drama Group.

DOUG: Drama Group?

ANN: Tuesdays and Thursdays. But after play practice, I'm
   yours.

DOUG: Go you Huskies . . .

DOUG *starts to exit and turns back.*

DOUG: And I might have something important to tell you . . .

ANN: What is it, a surprise?

DOUG: That's right . . .

They exit.

MORRIS: She coulda done better than him.

SPUD: It takes all kinds.

MORRIS: Zat what it takes? I always *wondered* what it took . . .

We hear the traffic light beeping from the street.

EXT. BOOKSHOP. DAY.

JOE, *pacing in front of the window. Theatrical sign in the window. Sign in the window: 'Out Will Return At . . . '* ANN *comes up to the door. Starts opening it with a key.*

JOE: I, excuse me, the sign says you'll be back at *two*. It's a
    quarter to *three* . . .

ANN *looks at the sign, changes the hand to read a quarter to three. She opens the door. Goes inside. He follows. Camera follows.*

INT. BOOKSTORE. DAY.

Old bookstore and stationery store. Several old typewriters for sale.

JOE (*of the sign*): You're doing a *play* . . .

ANN: Local Drama Group. (*she answers the phone*) Northern
    books. No it hasn't come in yet. As soon as it does. Yup,
    you too Marge.

She hangs up.

JOE: . . . small town. I suppose. You have to make your own
    fun.

ANN: Everybody makes their own fun. (*she answers another
    phone call*) F'you don't make it yourself, it ain't fun, it's

22

entertainment.

She picks up a half-knitted sweater off the computer.

ANN (*to phone while knitting*): Northern Books. (*to* JOE) What
    can I do for you?

JOE: I need a typewriter.

ANN: We got 'em. (*to phone*) North . . . No, Henry James was
    the novelist, Frank James was a criminal . . . (*to* JOE, *of
    the typewriter*) Yep, you came to the right place. (*to the
    phone*) Jesse James was the *brother*. (*Pause*) Of the
    novelist, that's right. That's all right Susie. See you
    tomorrow Susie –

JOE *has picked up a typewriter, old, manual.*

JOE: I want to rent this one.

ANN: Why don't you buy it, only forty bucks.

JOE: I have one, but they lost it.

ANN: Who?

JOE: The people in New Hampshire.

ANN (*shrugs*): That's why they have state borders . . . whyn't
    you get a replacement?

JOE: Well, it had sentimental value.

ANN: You buy the typewriter, I'll get it all spruced up, good
    as new. Better than new. It has some history.

JOE: Other one has history, too. I wrote my play on it.

ANN: You wrote a play on it, what play is that?

JOE: You haven't heard of it.

ANN: What's it called?

JOE: 'Anguish'.

Little kids enter to get candy. As JOE *speaks, he takes off his
regular glasses and puts on his reading glasses and inserts a piece*

23

of paper into the typewriter and types, 'Everyone makes their own fun – if you don't make it yourself, it's not fun, it's entertainment.'

ANN: 'Anguish' by Joseph Turner White . . . ?

JOE *looks up.*

ANN: You're Joseph Turner White?

JOE *switches glasses to look at her.*
MAUDE *comes in, goes back to the coffee machine.*

MAUDE: Afternoon Ann.

ANN *takes down a book from a shelf.*

ANN: Maude, this *man* wrote this *play!*
MAUDE: That a fact. Now, is it a good play.
ANN: Yes, Maude, it is. It is a *very* good play.
MAUDE: Well, then, what's he doing here?
ANN: What're you doing here . . . ?
JOE: Writing the movie.
MAUDE: You're writing the *movie* . . .
JOE: Yes.
MAUDE: What's it about?
JOE: It's about the quest for purity.

INT. WALT'S OFFICE. DAY.
WALT, BOB BARRENGER *and the* SCRIPT SUPERVISOR *are savaging the script.*

BOB: . . . because he wouldn't *say* that. Look: *(flips through the*
24

script, reads) 'Sister, I've just come from a fire. There's some things I want to think out . . . ' Now, come on, come on . . . 'Leave me *alone.*' A *gesture* . . . ? All right?

WALT *opens a case and extracts his lucky pillow which is embroidered 'Shoot first. Ask questions afterward.'*

WALT: What else?
BOB: Page . . . *three.* Now: 'It's a nice evening.' (*beat*) I'm not gonna say that . . . 'It's a nice . . . '

Knock on door.

WALT: Come in.

JOE *enters.*

WALT: Hey, Joe . . . Good. You know B . . .
JOE: I grew up on your mov . . .
BOB: Do you mind if I don't go through the usual bullshit about How I Loved It?

Knock on the door. CARLA *enters with another brown bag.*

BOB: I mean, okay, fine, but it's a motion *Picture.*
WALT: Thanks, honey, but, next time, bring two, save yourself a trip.
BOB: The people came to see a motion *Picture.* (*to* CARLA, *who's starting to leave*) . . . hold on . . .
WALT: He's saying, what are you saying, Bobby?
BOB: Tell it with . . .
WALT: Tell it with pictures.
BOB : Tell it with *pictures.* What I'm saying . . .
WALT: We've got three days to . . .

25

As BOB *talks, he exchanges glances with* CARLA.

BOB: You look at: girl comes in the room, an *apron*, a brown *bag*, what is she . . . ? She's a . . .

WALT: She's a . . .

BOB : She's a *waitress*.

WALT: What . . .

BOB: What I . . .

WALT: Hold on: what Bob is saying, you don't need . . .

BOB : You don't need 'Hi I've just come from the restaurant.'

WALT (*to* CARLA): You can go . . .

BOB: All right: Let's – (*he takes out a list,* CARLA *exits*) Page five, the fucking *horse* dies. (*of* CARLA) You know, *she* could be in the movie, she could, she's got a good face, she could be the Doctor's . . . uh, why does it have to be his, uh, *wife* . . . ? It could be his . . .

WALT: Bob, Bob, stick to the business, will you . . . ?

BOB : No, you're absolutely r . . .

WALT: And you go start with *that* stuff in *this* town . . .

BOB : Everybody needs a hobby. Okay, look page . . .

Knock at door. CLAIRE WELLESLEY *enters. The female star. Very sexual. Very serious. Around thirty. She looks in.*

WALT (*rising*): Claire, when did you . . .

CLAIRE: I just . . .

WALT: Claire, Bob Bar . . .

BOB : I saw *Desert Sun*, I wanna tell you . . .

CLAIRE: No, I was, I was, I was just *learning* on, it's a . . .

BOB : How'd you like working with Richard Hill?

CLAIRE: I loved it . . . he . . .

BOB : Isn't he a . . .

CLAIRE: It's . . .

WALT: We're just talking about the . . .

26

CLAIRE: Don't let me dis . . . I'll just . . .

WALT: No, no . . . Please.

BOB : I'm looking at page five: 'It's . . . '

JOE: 'It's a nice evening . . . '

WALT: This is Joe White.

CLAIRE: How can I thank you? How can I repay you for this part? It's a . . . what a, thank you for this part. The first scene at the Old Mill . . .

Pause.

WALT: Joe's been having some thoughts about the Old Mill Scene, Claire.

Pause.

CLAIRE: What, what's there to *think* about? (*Pause*) The scene's perfect . . . I, I get to say . . .

WALT: Yes, but, Joe, *Joe's* been, well, he's just been having a few, uh, 'Thoughts', about . . .

CLAIRE: How many times in your *life* do you get a speech like that?

WALT: Yeah.

CLAIRE: This scene is why I'm doing the movie. 'Look at the mill, Frank – look at the way it goes around . . . *half* of the time the darned wheel's under water, but . . . '

WALT: Yes, yes, but . . .

CLAIRE: ' . . . but still it rises up . . . It rises up, Frank, high as it can go.'

WALT: Yeah. Joe? Would you, uh, tell Claire, the, uh, the 'thoughts' you've been . . .

Pause.

EXT. STATE AND MAIN. DAY.

Angle on ANN, *who is putting up posters of the play. She sighs and walks forward, into* JOE, *who is waiting at the traffic light, his bag on the ground beside him.*

ANN (*of typewriter*): All ready to go!

JOE *nods. Looks down at her posterior.*

JOE: So young, so unlined, so full of promise. (*Pause*) So innocent.
ANN: I beg your pardon?

JOE *extracts the book of his she had in her back pocket. He looks at his photo on the back cover. They start to cross the street.*

JOE: I quit.
ANN: You quit.
JOE: I quit the movie.
ANN: Why did you quit?
JOE: Actually, I'm not sure if I quit. I think that I got fired. I'm such a liar. I never could tell the truth.
ANN: Don't be hard on yourself.
JOE: I just got kicked off my first movie.
ANN: Well. Everybody has reversals. If you were never down how would you know when you were up?
JOE: That's good. That's really good. You have a gift for words.
ANN: It's in your play.

She holds up 'Anguish'.

JOE: You like my play.
ANN: Yes.

JOE: Why?

ANN: It's about life.

JOE: Could you tell me when's the next train?

ANN: N'about ten minutes. What was your movie about?

They stop by the park bench.
Pause.

ANN: No, of course, you don't want to talk about it.

JOE (*hands her the script*): It's about a man who gets a second
chance.

The cop (CAL) *passes.*

CAL: Evening, Annie.

ANN: Evening, Cal. (*to* JOE) Would you tell me about it?

JOE: I . . .

ANN: No, of course, you want to get out of town.

JOE: It's . . .

He starts to walk, she puts the typewriter down on the ground.
JOE *hesitates. He puts the script under the typewriter. Pause. He*
shakes his head.

ANN: It's okay . . .

They walk on.

EXT. SPORTING GOODS STORE. DAY.
The OWNER *is closing up.*

OWNER: Evening, Annie. See you at rehearsal.

ANN: You know your line?

OWNER: 'Rise, one need not bend the knee before the throne of justice.'

ANN: Go you Huskies.

OWNER *walks away.*

JOE (*of the clothing on the rack*): They leave it out all night?

He tries on a jacket. One sleeve is one foot shorter than the other.

ANN: Not worth stealing. Only thing in town worth something, stained glass window.

She gestures at the firehouse.

JOE: Ever wonder why the dalmatian's the symbol of the firehouse?

ANN: First organized fire department was on the border of Dalmatia and Sardinia in the year 642.

JOE: But why the dalmatian?

ANN: It was either that, or a sardine.

JOE *nods. Beat. He looks down at the jacket with one sleeve too short.*

ANN: You get what you pay for.

JOE: That's true. You grow up here?

ANN: Central High, 'n' matinees, the Bijou Theatre.

They walk past the firehouse. ANN *gives a dog biscuit to the firedog who runs out of the firehouse to her.*

JOE: Nice town.

Beat. He gets a bit choked up.

ANN: You want to talk about it?

JOE *shakes his head. They walk off.*

EXT. RAILROAD CROSSING. DAY.

JOE: . . . that . . . that he *prayed* for a second chance. But . . . do you see?

ANN: Yes.

JOE: That, he says, there *are* no second chances . . . that he's been presented what he *prayed* for . . . and: he's ruined it.

ANN: Yes . . .

JOE: But, but but but...

ANN: No, no, I see . . .

JOE: That: in an act of . . .

ANN: Yes . . .

JOE: Of *mercy* . . . of . . .

ANN: I understand . . .

JOE: . . . that . . . he *sees* that . . .

ANN: As the Old Mill goes around . . .

JOE: Of course, of course that's what I'm *saying*. As the Old Mill goes around, he *sees* . . .

ANN: Of course.

JOE: . . . that it has been vouchsafed to him.

ANN: That's, that's, that's, that's beautiful . . .

JOE: And you're the only one who'll ever hear that speech. (*pause*) Just you.

Beat. They stop and look at each other. Beat. A railroad crossingbar comes down behind them, as we hear the DINGING and realize we are at a railroad crossing.

31

ANN: Well. It was a pleasure meeting you.
JOE: And likewise.
ANN: Goodbye.
JOE: Goodbye.

Pause.
We see the train pass in the background. We hear the train
whistling. It's way off.

ANN (*pause*): Next train innt for two hours.

They walk on away from the station. In the background we see
the STATIONMASTER. *He and* ANN *wave. They walk past the*
shingle for DOC WILSON.

ANN: So that the Old Mill, the Old *Mill* represents . . . the
   wheel of fate ... is that too . . .
JOE: No, no. Of course, that's *exactly* what it represents . . .
ANN: That whole . . .

They walk on together and find themselves on a residential street.

EXT. ANN'S HOME. DUSK
JOE *and* ANN *are walking. They stop in front of an old*
picketfence house with a porch swing.

JOE: The, the, the, the *sanctity* of everyday things . . .
ANN: Everyday things . . . yes.
JOE: For example, he's just come back from a *fire* and he . . .
   um . . . (*he shakes his head*) That's a fine house. You look
   at that, and you know, there's nice people that live there.
ANN: I live there.
JOE: Really. With the porch swing and everything . . .

32

ANN: Surest thing you know.

Pause.

JOE: I don't mean to impose, but . . . do you think we
   might . . .
ANN: That's what the swing is *there* for . . .

They walk onto the porch, and sit on the swing.

JOE: (*to himself*) . . . that's what the swing is *there* for . . . that
   its *purpose, isn't* it . . .
ANN: . . . I always thought so . . .

They swing back and forth. The swing creaks.

JOE: . . . such a pleasant sound.
ANN: Mmm.
JOE: 'Cause, 'cause, it's . . . it's the *simple* things, that . . .
ANN: Yes . . .
JOE: . . . that

DOUG *walks up.*

DOUG: Waal, *there* you are, and Have I Got Some News for
   You . . .
ANN: Doug, this is Joe White, and this is, this, this is my
   fiancé, Doug Mac . . .
JOE: S'a pleasure.
DOUG: *Guess* who is THIS CLOSE to a nomination to State
   Senate . . . which is *this close to one step from Congress!*
ANN: . . . who . . . ?
JOE: Well, I guess I'll . . . get down to the station. It was lovely
   meeting . . .

ANN: Mr White is . . .

DOUG: (*as he takes* ANN *toward the door*) Nice meeting you
. . . they were, let me tell you, they were a bit coy at first,
I told them: Look: the people are *tired*, they're going to
vote their pocketbook, *yes*, but . . .

JOE *walks off and exchanges glances with* ANN, *who lingers
behind. She pushes the porch swing and exits. As it swings,* JOE
watches.

INT. TRAIN STATION. NIGHT.

JOE *enters with his bag. He stands looking at the long poster
reading 'Waterford, Home of the Huskies, Division Champions,
1971, 1972, 1974, 1975, 1976'.*
Beat.
JOE *is looking at the banner, when the old* STATIONMASTER
enters.

JOE: . . . what happened in 1973?

Beat. The STATIONMASTER *looks around, and leans in to* JOE,
confidentially.
The door opens. It is WALT. *The* STATIONMASTER *retreats.*
WALT *comes forward.*

WALT: Don't run off. Don't run off, we *need* you. You know
why? You're why we're here. Your script is why we're
here . . . (*of bag*) Gimme that. Big deal. We fight a little
bit? You show me a family that doesn't. But we got
something special. What is it? We're here to make a
movie. Can't use the Old Mill. Well, that happens. What
you got to do, you find the *essence* – what was it, that
brought us here. It wasn't the building Joe, it was an

34

idea. It was an essence – what is the essence of your story? Joe?

Pause.

JOE: It's about a man who gets a second chance.
WALT: Then, you *write* that. And then this is *our* second chance. That's why we're here . . .

Pause.

JOE: I want to make a good film.
WALT: I know you do.
JOE: And maybe it will be a better movie without the old mill, I . . .
WALT: Hey, it's with the Gods. We don't have the money, we have to write it out. The best or not. (*shrugs*) And that's a lesson. You get your typewriter yet . . . ?
JOE: Um, no.

WALT *picks up cell phone, dials. Lights of train go by outside.*
STATIONMASTER *enters and calls the train.*

WALT (*into phone*): Grace, get on the other phone, call that girl: well, call her, and have whatsername send up some *nosh* . . . what do you like to drink . . . ?
JOE: I don't drink.
WALT: Did my matzohs come? Get some for everybody. (*into phone*) Thank you. (*hangs up phone*) Lemme tell you about my first movie . . .

EXT. BOOKSTORE. DAY.
The PRODUCTION ASSISTANT *is stapling a casting notice for*

35

'The Old Mill' half over the notice of the amateur theatricals poster. DOUG *shows up, looks in the window. Looks at poster, takes it down, looks around.*
Angle: the park bench. ANN, *her feet up on the old typewriter, is sitting, reading the script.* DOUG *comes up.*

DOUG: What, what, what are you doing here?
ANN: Yes, that's right.
DOUG: Look at this. Do you know what they're offering? Look at this. They treat us like we're their backyard. Do you know what they're offering for three days to close down Main Street?
ANN: What are they offering?
DOUG: Ten thousand dollars.
ANN: That's so beautiful . . .
DOUG: I beg your pardon?

ANN *gestures at the script.*

ANN: 'The mill grinds the grain, but the grain is not destroyed. *Although* it is altered . . . '
DOUG: Sure, but . . . ten thousand dollars. Do you know what they . . . this movie is budgeted at fifty *million* dol . . . they're coming up here, offer us a measl . . .

INT. MAYOR'S HOME. DAY.
The Mayor's wife (SHERRY) *comes into the room. Her hands are full of lists, giving instructions to a handyman.*

SHERRY: The chairs go, the Lazyboy goes . . .
MAYOR: . . . not the Lazyboy . . .

CAL, *the policeman, enters, carrying an old spinning wheel.*

CAL: Hi, Sherry . . .

SHERRY: . . . put it in the living-room . . . and we have
thirteen at table.

MAYOR: . . . we don't have thirteen at table . . .

SHERRY: Bob Barrenger, Claire Wellesley, the *director* . . .

MAYOR: Waal, then, invite someone *else*, then . . .

SHERRY: I don't want to invite someone else, because this is
the *most exclusive* . . .

MAYOR: Waal, then, you know, you do whatever would make
you happy. Sher. This is your party, and whatever . . .

DOUG *enters.* CAL *exits carrying a pinball machine.*

CAL: Hi Doug.

DOUG: Cal. I want a city council meeting.

MAYOR: . . . little woman has gone crazy about our dinner
party . . . City Council . . . ? What's the trouble . . . ?

DOUG: Main Street.

MAYOR (*sighs*): Doug, the traffic light . . .

DOUG: *Fuck* the traffic light. I'm talking about three percent
of the adjusted gross of a Major Motion Picture . . .

EXT. PARK. DAY.
JOE *walks up.* ANN *is standing there.*

JOE: Hi.

ANN (*simultaneously*): What are you doing? (*pause*) I love
your script.

JOE: (*simultaneously*) They decided, I decided to, to . . . You
love what?

ANN: You're still here.

JOE: I . . . I decided to give it another chhh . . .

ANN: I love your script.

Pause.

JOE: What?

POSTMAN (*as he delivers mail to her*): Mornin', Annie . . .

ANN: See you at rehearsal tonight?

POSTMAN: 'In the name of justice, Sir, I bid you pause. For she is our Queen . . . '

POSTMAN *exits.*

JOE: In fact, in fact, in fact, I'm not sure if I'm giving *them* a second chance, or they're giving it to me. That's the truth. The truth's best, don't you think?

ANN: You'd know bettern me.

JOE: How can you *say* that?

ANN: It's in your script . . . it's about getting a second chance. Innit? 'You *can* go back . . . '

JOE: I *can*?

ANN: You bet your life. (*refers to script*) 'The mill wheel goes around . . . some times it's even under water – then it rises up, as high as it can go . . . '

JOE: But how do I . . . how do I do a film called 'The Old Mill', when I don't have an old mill?

ANN: Well, first, you got to change the title . . .

INT. PRODUCTION OFFICE. DAY.

Sign reads 'days till shoot . . . 3'.

WALT *is on the phone. Covers the phone. Crossed sticks on the wall.* WALT *plays with a shuffleboard discus.*

GIRL PRODUCTION ASSISTANT *brings cup of coffee to* WALT. *Her t-shirt reads, 'Does it have to be an old mill . . . ?'*

WALT: (*to* FIRST ASSISTANT DIRECTOR) No, he doesn't want

to work out with the Waterford Huskies . . . Because he's
Bob Barrenger . . . Call up his girl in Aspen, have em
ship his weight . . . Yeah, well, fine, he's not gonna do
the Pond scene, unless he can work out. Call up his girl
in Aspen, and have her ship the weights out . . .

WALT *hangs up the phone.* SECRETARY *enters with folders that
she hands to* WALT.

WALT: Who designed these costumes? Who designed these
    costumes. It looks like Edith Head puked and that *puke*
    designed these costumes. Get Madge.
SECRETARY (*to* FIRST ASSISTANT DIRECTOR): Your wife is
    on the phone.
WALT: I *have* no wife.

A PRODUCTION ASSISTANT *comes in with a big bakery box.
They open it to show it is a huge loaf of bread, and on it is
written, in bread, 'Waterford Welcomes The Old Mill'.*

WALT (*calling out*): We need a new name for the movie.
    Where's the writer?
UBERTO: (*entering with storyboards*) Wally, I got to takes out
    that window from the dog. I can't shoot through . . .

*Camera moves on past the production board, where we see
'Dinner with the Mayor' in red. And the* COSTUME DESIGNER
comes up.

COSTUME DESIGNER: . . . Claire's got a problem.
UBERTO: Wally, if I hafes a moment of your time . . . look at
    these storyboards. THIS SHOT, I can't shoot this shot,
    you want.
WALT: Why?

UBERTO: Because they gots a window with a dogs in it. You want me to 'push in'. Or I can lose the shot.

WALT: No you can't lose the shot. The meaning of the *film* is in that shot.

UBERTO: But, Wally, the window of the *firehut* . . .

WALT: I don't care. *Fix* it.

WALT *goes into confab with the* COSTUME DESIGNER.

WALT (*of sketches*): You show Claire these sketches?

COSTUME DESIGNER: Yes.

WALT: Did she throw up?

COSTUME DESIGNER: That isn't very nice.

WALT: Oh, really, then why don't you sue me in the World Court. Did she like the costumes?

COSTUME DESIGNER: I can't tell.

WALT: Why not?

COSTUME DESIGNER: She won't stop crying . . .

WALT (*to* FIRST ASSISTANT DIRECTOR): Find out when Marty Rossen's arriving, get him a bunch of lilacs to send to the broad.

FIRST A D: Town's out of lilacs.

WALT: You go in her room, take the lilacs from the water, dry them. Go buy some cellophane, wrap 'em up, and get a card from *Marty*. (*to* costume designer) What's her problem?

COSTUME DESIGNER: She doesn't want to Bare Her Breasts.

WALT: She Doesn't Want to Bare Her Breasts . . . what, in the Nude Scene . . . ? What are we paying her three mil?

COSTUME DESIGNER: – she's got 'religion'.

WALT: Her religion bars her from fulfilling her contr . . .

Camera follows WALT *to the sound of crying.*
We hear crying from the next room. WALT *opens the door quietly.*

WALT: Claire . . . ? Claire . . . ? (*to* UBERTO) Just figure out
    how to take the shot. Claire . . . Claire . . . ? It's Wally.
    (*pause*) May I come in . . . ?

Beat. He motions his entourage to stand back.

INT. PRODUCTION OFFICE – WASHROOM. DAY.
WALT *enters the room. Camera follows.*
WALT (*softly*): What is it, pal . . . ?

Pause. CLAIRE *mumbles.*

WALT: What . . . ?
CLAIRE: I can't do it, Walt.
WALT: You can't do what?
CLAIRE: It isn't *right*. I can't . . . I . . . I know I si . . . I, they, I
    don't know if they told me it was in the con . . .
WALT: *Forget* the contract. Claire. What is it?
CLAIRE: I don't want to take my shirt off in that con . . . What
    are these things that they're asking of me . . . ? Wha . . .
    wha . . . wha . . . I try to be good: the only thing I care
    about is . . .
WALT: *I* know that . . .
CLAIRE: Is . . . is the Movie!

As they talk, the ASSISTANT DIRECTORS *come in and hand him
sheets to approve.*

WALT: I know that, Claire. I, we *all* know . . .
CLAIRE: Everybody, they, they, they treat me like a . . .
WALT: . . . *no*, they don't . . .
CLAIRE: . . . they treat me like a *child*. I, I . . . to bare my *body*.
WALT: Now, look. Claire: Listen to me – (*he takes her hand in*

his) I want to tell you a story.

The door to her room opens. A PRODUCTION ASSISTANT *brings in a bunch of lilacs, hands them to Walt.*

WALT: Fuck flowers, we aren't talking about flowers, we're talking about a human being.

CLAIRE: I . . . I . . .

WALT: Who are these from?

PRODUCTION ASSISTANT: Marty.

WALT: Well that's very thoughtful of him. Eleonora Duse . . .

CLAIRE: . . . I can't do it, Wally . . .

WALT: Listen to me: Eleonora *Duse* was playing Hamlet in London in 1905, and Royalty could not get a ticket. She said, 'I'm not doing the seven shows a week I signed for.' She said, 'I cannot bare my soul seven times a week. I am an artist. I'll do four shows a week.' (*pause*) The greatest actress of her time. You know what her Producer said?

CLAIRE (*pause, softly*): What?

WALT: Nothing. He held her and he wept. Because he . . .

CLAIRE: . . . I . . .

WALT: Because he understood. That was her life's blood on the stage.

CLAIRE *nods, breaks into sobs.*

WALT: . . . I know . . . I know . . .

CLAIRE (*pause*): . . . and, and, and did she . . . ? and she did the seven shows . . .

WALT: No, she didn't Claire. But I think you should do this scene.

SECRETARY *comes in with memos and* WALT *deals with them,*

while comforting CLAIRE.

Beat. CLAIRE *sobs. She shakes her head. She brings herself under control.*

CLAIRE: Wally . . .
WALT: I know, I know.

He puts his arm around her, starts walking toward the door.

WALT: I know, it's the hardest thing in the world, and it
    seems everybody wants . . .
CLAIRE: . . . yes . . .
WALT: . . . wants a piece . . .
CLAIRE: Yes.
WALT: And you know what . . . ?
CLAIRE: We, we have to give it.
WALT (*nods*): . . . and my heart goes out to you, because I
    know . . .

INT. PRODUCTION OFFICE – BACK ROOM. DAY.
WALT *opens the door. We hear the* FIRST ASSISTANT
DIRECTOR *and the* COSTUME DESIGNER *chatting outside the door, as they walk out.*

WALT: That, that's *your* life's blood on the st . . .
FIRST A D: I don't know what she's bitching about, she's
    flashed her tits in the last five movies . . . she'd bare her
    breasts to do a *voice* over.

Camera follows WALT *and* CLAIRE *out. A tableau of the four of them. The* FIRST ASSISTANT DIRECTOR *drinking coffee, sees he has been overheard. Beat.* CLAIRE *starts soundlessly heaving, sobbing. She goes 'Oh!' as if she has just been hit in the stomach,*

43

falls back into the room, closes the door. Sobbing sounds emanate.

FIRST A D: I . . .

WALT: Get Mitch Cohn on the phone in New York, tell him
    she's breaking her contract and we're very up . . .

FIRST A D: I . . .

WALT: We're very upset with her. Get someone to *double for
    her,* her tits, the tits scene, call LA. I want to see some
    pictures of the women's *tits*. Of their *tits*.

FIRST A D: I'm very sorry I . . .

WALT: You're very sorry, you passive aggressive, son-of-a-
    bitch . . . can we replace him?

BILL: We start shooting in three days.

COSTUME DESIGNER: You want to see the fireman's
    costumes? . . . 'cause I found this moleskin for the collar,
    it's not black, but it *looks* black . . . It's not *brown*, but . . .

SECRETARY: Marty Rossen's touched down.

EXT. PARK BENCH. DAY.

ANN *and* JOE *sit on a bench. He is looking at her as she finishes
the script. Tears in her eyes. She closes the cover.*

JOE (*beat*): What I need to *say*...

ANN: *Yes* . . .

JOE: About *conflict* . . .

ANN: That's why you didn't want to take the *Mill* out . . .
    you've . . .

JOE: . . . the, the, the symbol of the fire . . .

ANN: The *firehouse* . . .

JOE: I . . .

ANN: But but but but but it's better *without* -

JOE: *How* . . . ?

ANN: Wait wait wait wait wait, he gets a second chance, do

44

you see? And *you* get a second chance!

JOE: No, I don't . . .

ANN (*as she holds the script*): He doesn't go back to the *mill*, he gets a second chance to go back to the *firehouse* . . .

JOE *takes off one pair of glasses and changes them for another.*

ANN: You don't *need* the Mill. This is what (*she gestures at the script*) you see: this is what you're, this is what the script is *saying* . . . (*a person walks by*) Hi Emma, see you tonight?

EMMA *waves and nods.*

ANN: This is, look... (*to* EMMA) Go you Huskies. (*to* JOE) . . . what *I* see you saying, is: you have the two elements, Fire and *Water*. The firehouse, and the *Old Mill* . . . Do you know, you could . . .

JOE: What are you doing tonight?

ANN: Me?

JOE: Yes.

JOE *and* ANN *walk down the street. As they do so they are passed by the airport van.*

ANN: Tonight, tonight, I . . . I have play practice . . .

JOE: . . . Oh . . . Oh. Well. That's very important.

EXT. HOTEL STEPS. DAY.
WALT *and the* FIRST ASSISTANT DIRECTOR *come down the steps to meet the arriving airport van. It stops.* MARTY ROSSEN *gets out.* WALT *hands his bags to a* PRODUCTION ASSISTANT.

WALT: Marteleh, vos macht a yid . . . ?

He hands MARTY *the breadloaf.* MARTY *takes a bite.*

MARTY: You cool the broad out?
WALT: I left that for you.
MARTY: That's thoughtful. (*of the bread*) Ziz good, you try
    this?

As they speak a PRODUCTION ASSISTANT *is unloading Marty's*
high-end luggage from the van.

WALT: Oh yeah, I'm really gonna eat carbohydrates . . .
MARTY: (*of the town*) What'd you do, *build* this . . . ?
WALT: How was your flight?
MARTY: We're flying over pigs, we're flying over *sheep* . . .
WALT: Did you bring Bob's weights?
MARTY: They're coming Fedex . . .
WALT: (*of the bags*) What's in all the bags?
MARTY: My undies, 'cause, you can't get this picture off on
    time I'm gonna wet myself.
WALT: I'm gonna bring it off.
MARTY: 55 days and I take home the camera. I got an idea
    for a *product* placement . . .

They start up the stairs when DOC WILSON *walks by. Girl on a*
scooter (SALLY) *scooting the other way, her arm in a cast.*
MARTY *and* WALT *turn back to watch on the steps, under the*
awning.
CARLA *walks through carrying food bags.*

DOC WILSON: Hiya Sally . . .
SALLY: Hiya Doc . . .
DOC WILSON: How's the arm?

SALLY: Still itchin'.

DOC WILSON: Good! A sign it's getting well.

MARTY: (of scene) Stop . . .

WALT: That's what I said.

MARTY: How are you getting on with these fine people?

WALT: Like dykes and dogs.

INT. BOB'S ROOM. DAY.

BOB *is doing Tai Chi. Knock on the door. He goes to it, opens it.*
CARLA *is bringing him his dinner.*

BOB: Yeah. Come in.

CARLA *comes in.*

BOB: I'm just . . .

*She puts his dinner down on the coffee table. He takes out money
from his pants to pay her.*

CARLA: The prices are going up.

BOB: But, that's the way of the world, huh? Everybody's gotta
    eat. Way of the world.

*He sits before his dinner, hands her some money. Remembers
himself.*

BOB: Well, I'm pretty impolite. Would you like some?

CARLA: I don't eat vegetables.

BOB: Well, I can offer you something to drink?

CARLA: Sure, what have you got?

BOB: What do you drink?

CARLA: Bourbon and milk.

BOB: How old are you?

CARLA: (*whispers to him*)

BOB *makes her a drink out of his fridge, hands it to her.*

BOB: Then I hope you wouldn't tell anyone that I gave you
    this.

CARLA: I wouldn't tell anyone anything that happened
    between me and somebody who was my friend.

Pause.

BOB: Nice town that you've got here.

CARLA: You want to see it better, we could go out on the
    roof.

BOB: . . . wouldn't that be dangerous?

CARLA: . . . not if you've got something to hold on to.

EXT. MAIN STREET. DUSK.

JOE *is walking down the street. A script in his hand, scribbling.*

UBERTO *walks next to him.*

UBERTO: Because if you cannot tells me what is it, how I,
    how does I take a *pictures* of it? Wally wants me, push in
    through the weendow . . .

JOE *is scribbling in the script.*

JOE: Yeah, no, can I . . . if you'd excuse me, I've just got
    to . . .

JOE *walks away and the camera takes him into a backyard, by a
bunch of clotheslines. His glasses fall apart as he changes them.*

48

He looks up as the wind blows the sheet.
He sees ANN, *sitting on the backstairs of what, as we draw closer,*
we see is the playhouse. In back of her we see the 'Trials of the
Heart' flats, seen from the back.
Angle: his POV.

ANN: Hello.
JOE: I thought you had play practice.
ANN: Don't look good for 'Trials of the Heart'.
JOE: Well, then, it don't look good for the Huskies . . .
ANN: That's for sure.

They walk down the street. As they walk down the street, the dog
comes over and ANN *throws him his biscuit over her shoulder.*

JOE: What happened?
ANN: Cast stood me up.
JOE: Uh huh.
ANN: They're all preparing for the auditions – your movie.

JOE *gets an idea, and trades glasses, one pair for the other. He*
kneels.

ANN: 'Rise, one need not bend the knee before the throne of
     justice.'
JOE: What?
ANN: What are you doing down there?
JOE: My glasses fell apart. I lost the . . .
ANN: . . . lost the screw . . .
JOE: You got a paperclip?

A LITTLE KID *is walking by, carrying a fishing rod.*

LITTLE KID: Evening, Annie.

ANN: Evenin', sweetheart.

LITTLE KID: Go you Huskies.

ANN: You said it.

JOE: You like kids?

ANN: Never saw the point of 'em.

JOE: Me, too. You have a paperclip?

ANN: Paperclip?

JOE: Fix my glasses.

ANN: Better idea . . .

ANN *ducks under the sheet hanging by the door. She and* JOE
come upon a FISHERWOMAN *who is standing by the bank about
to make a cast.*
We see ANN *take some leader from the woman and burn one end
to make a hinge.*

JOE: Gonna be good as new.

ANN: Better'n new, cause it's got a *story*. Want to do the
    other part?

JOE *takes the hinge and a match and tries to fix the hinge, and
burns his finger.*

JOE: Ow.

JOE *grabs for the nearest object. Pause.*

ANN: What?

JOE *shows her.*

ANN : Y'know what you got there? You got a fishhook in
    your finger.

EXT. BOOKSTORE. DUSK.

DOUG *standing, holding a bunch of flowers. The* FIRST
ASSISTANT DIRECTOR *walks by. Looks in the window.*

FIRST A D: I'm looking for the writer.

DOUG: What the hell are *you* so down about?

FIRST A D (*pause*): My wife's going to have a baby.

DOUG: How about that.

FIRST A D: Mmmm. (*Pause*) You have children?

DOUG: No. (*pause*) No, but we're planning to.

FIRST A D: (*pause*) Could you tell me where a fellow goes to
    get a drink in this town?

DOUG: Yes.

INT. WALT'S HOTEL ROOM. NIGHT.

MARTY *and* WALT *et al. studying various documents.* CLAIRE
sitting there.

MARTY: I want to tell you something, Wally, he's a pussycat.
    My thing is to see everybody does what they said they
    would and I have to do that. Now: what is this you want
    Eight Hundred Thousand Dollars to do what you're being
    paid to, you already *signed* you'd do . . . ? (*pause*) What
    is that?

CLAIRE: I think I should talk to my agent, Marty, you and I
    should, we should, really not discuss . . .

MARTY: Who is her agent . . . ?

BILL: Mitch Cohn . . .

CLAIRE: He's . . .

MARTY: Get him on the phone.

CLAIRE: He's on the Island, he'll be back on . . .

MARTY: Get him on the . . .

CLAIRE *starts back to her room.*

MARTY: I want you to hear this.
CLAIRE: I really think that *business* . . . matters should be discussed between you t . . .
MARTY: Well, I'm going to discuss 'em between you babe, 'cause it's your idea, and you think you're going to sign to do a, then hold us up in the *wilds* sweetheart, you are in *error* . . .

BILL *hands him the phone.*

BILL: He's on the ph . . .
MARTY (*takes phone*): Mitch, Marty Rossen, I'm here in . . .
BILL: Wat . . .
MARTY: I'm somewhere in the, I'm on location, eh. This . . . well I'm going to solve it here, or this *Bimbo* you sent me's going to be doing a fuckin' *donkey* act in Akron, I'm talking about Restraint of Trade, Breach of . . . IT'S VERY SIMPLE . . . !

JOE *enters. His finger bandaged.*

JOE: (*tentatively*) Hi!
MARTY: Her tits! Her tits! How, that she signed IN HER CONTRACT, we hired her 'cause of ten years at the Actors Studio, the way she played *Medea*? . . . Her last two pictures laid there on the screen like my first *wife* . . .
CLAIRE (*starts to cry*): You have no right to . . .
MARTY: Cool it, babe, you started this . . .
JOE: What's the . . .
WALT: Where have you been . . . ?
MARTY: You tell me: you tell me *now*, I've got to *shoot* on Wednesday and I will *not* pay your Blood Money and

52

PS, pal, I put the word out on the street and Betty Boop can look for work in *squigglevision* . . .

CLAIRE *starts to get up.*

MARTY: *Siddown*!

JOE: I really don't think you should be talking this way to a lady.

MARTY: . . . would you excuse me, please . . .

CLAIRE: You can't treat me like this. I'm not a child!

JOE: She's absolutely r . . .

CLAIRE: I'm not a *child* . . . I have *feelings* . . . Don't you . . . don't, don't . . . don't . . .

CLAIRE *exits crying.*

MARTY: (*his suitcase next to him – to phone*) Well, you call him, and call me back, but this is it, pal, you *fuck* with me, and I'm going to tear out your heart and piss on your lungs through the hole in your *chest*. And the best to Marion . . . (*beat, he hangs up, to* JOE) Where have *you* been?

JOE: I . . .

MARTY: He says they're looking for you all day, you're on *salary*, he needs *pages*, what are you, you been 'haying'? Now –

WALT: Marty . . .

MARTY: Later for that, Walt, let's get this: we need the 'pages' for the new 'Old Mill' . . . all right? We need a new title, we need a . . .

BILL: Rewrites that Bob Barrenger requested . . . the Dead Horse Scene, the . . .

MARTY: Whatever it is. Go *do* it. How you doing on the permit?

WALT: It's just a formality.

MARTY: That's why I *want* it. (*to* JOE) Type it up and get it back to me in . . .

JOE: I can't.

WALT: Why?

MARTY: You can't write it?

JOE: I can write it. I can't type it.

WALT: Why?

JOE: I hurt my finger.

WALT: Get a typist. Gettim a typist. Get outta here.

JOE *exits. They turn to survey the board.*

MARTY: Eight hundred grand to show her tits . . .

WALT: *Pay* her.

MARTY: I don't got the money.

WALT: Find the money.

MARTY: I got a company . . . give us a million dollars, put their product in the film.

WALT (*looking at a paper* MARTY *hands him*): No no no no no no no no no find me the money . . .

INT. JOE'S ROOM. NIGHT.

JOE *takes out paper, looks around. Sighs. Picks up phone, calls desk.*

JOE (*into phone*): This is Joe White, in . . . six ten, they're sending up a *typist*?

He takes out a sheet of foolscap and a pencil, starts to write. A knock at the door.

JOE (*into phone*): Okay, I thank you. It's here.

54

JOE *hangs up the phone, goes to the door, opens it. It is* CLAIRE.

CLAIRE: You said, 'You can't talk that way to a lady . . . ', you stood up for me. (*beat*) What do you have to drink?

She looks around. Sees a gift basket containing a bottle of Stolichnaya and a box of matzoh, wrapped with a 'Welcome Back' ribbon.

CLAIRE: Matzoh! Are you Jewish?
JOE: I, actually yes.
CLAIRE: I love Jewish men.
JOE: Why?
CLAIRE: *You* know . . . Where's your bathroom?

CLAIRE *goes into the bathroom.*

JOE: You liked the script, huh . . . ?

EXT. MAIN STREET. NIGHT.
ANN *sitting on the park bench, holding the lure.*

DOUG (*still carrying bouquet of flowers*): Where have you been?

DOUG *gives* ANN *the bouquet.*

ANN: Hi!
DOUG: We had a date.
ANN: We did . . . ?
DOUG: Where have you been . . .
ANN: I've been thinking.
DOUG: Where have you been, we had a date for *three* . . .

55

where have you *been* . . . ?

ANN: I have to tell you something . . .

DOUG: Well, I *know*, because they *told* me you were with that writer from the, you see, this is what I mean, the whole *town* has been warped by the, by, by the presence of the movie company, they holler, and we jump, you have a *date*, they call, you're doing business nine o'clock at night, it isn't . . .

ANN: I wasn't doing business.

DOUG: Oh. What were you doing, then, that's so important that you shouldn't call your fian . . .

ANN: It's all over between us, Doug, I'm sorry, but that's the truth. I've found someone else, and, it's very serious and it's the end. I'm sorry. (*pause*) It isn't *you*, j . . .

DOUG: Wai . . . It's so serious you couldn't call to tell me you'd be . . . what . . . ? What did you say . . . ?

ANN: It's all over between us. (*pause*) I've found someone else.

DOUG (*pause*): Let me review here: You're . . . what are you . . . you've . . . it's all over between us . . . ?

ANN: I'm sorry.

DOUG: Who is this person that you've found?

ANN (*pause*): He works on the movie.

DOUG: No. Don't tell me that.

ANN: I'm sorry.

DOUG: Why, you *whore*!

DOUG *starts to cry*. FIRST ASSISTANT DIRECTOR *shows up*.

FIRST A D: Can you type?

ANN: Never admit you can type.

FIRST A D: If you can type, they need you over at the hotel.

INT. JOE'S HOTEL ROOM. NIGHT.
JOE *is standing by the side of the bed, holding Claire's clothes,*
trying to induce her to put them on. CLAIRE *is sitting on the side*
of the bed, naked.

JOE: Look.
CLAIRE: I feel so *close* to you . . .
JOE: Look, look, I like you *very much* . . .
CLAIRE: I like you, too.
JOE: But not that *way* . . .
CLAIRE: But we . . .
JOE: Look, look, there's someone else . . .

Sound of a knock on the door.

JOE: Great. Who is it . . . ?
ANN: 'Room service!'
JOE: (*to* CLAIRE) Would you go in . . .

JOE *gestures to the bathroom. He hands* CLAIRE *her clothes.*

JOE: Would you put on your cl . . . (*to door*) Just leave it
    outside.
ANN: You have to sign for it.

INT. HALL. NIGHT.
ANN *hurriedly arranging the flowers in the platen of the*
typewriter. From inside the room we hear JOE's *voice: 'Alright,*
one moment!' He opens the door.

ANN: I'm gonna be your typist for this evening.
JOE: Oh God . . .
ANN: And here's some hydrogen peroxide.

57

JOE: I don't drink.
ANN: It's for your finger.
JOE: One moment.

JOE *closes the door.*

IINT. JOE'S ROOM. NIGHT.
CLAIRE *is still sitting on the bed, has a lit cigarette. Poured herself a drink.* JOE *goes over to her, thrusts her clothes onto her.*

JOE: You have to hide.
CLAIRE: Who is that . . . ?
JOE: That's my . . .
CLAIRE: Oh.
JOE: Will you help me out . . . ?
CLAIRE: I . . .

JOE *hustles back to the door. Opens the door.* ANN *is still standing there with the typewriter.*

JOE: Hi.
ANN: You going to ask me in?

JOE *looks back over his shoulder.*

ANN: Thought you might like this.
JOE (*he takes the flowers*): Thank you.
ANN: Read the card.
JOE (*reads*): 'To the love of my life. Love, Doug'?
ANN: The other side.
JOE: Oh.

He turns the card over.

ANN: Don't you think you should put them in water?

JOE: Why?

ANN: . . . because if you don't, they die . . .

ANN *goes into the bathroom, fills up the vase. Comes out.*

ANN: Shouldn't we start?

Pause.

JOE: Start? This isn't a good time.

ANN: Oh. That's all right. Then I'll come back at a better
time. What would be a better time?

JOE: Later on.

ANN: Then I'll come back, then.

JOE: You, um, you, um, you going out with your fiancé?

ANN: No, I just broke up with him. I'll see you tomorrow.

ANN *starts to exit.*

INT. TAVERN INN HALLWAY. NIGHT.
ANN *digs in pocket, takes out the lure we previously saw in Joe's
finger. She reenters the room.*

ANN: It occurred to me, you'd wanna have this: sort of a
memento of our . . .

Angle, in the room. CLAIRE *is standing there, basically naked.
Pause.*

CLAIRE: Hi. I hope I'm not disturbing . . .

JOE: She came in here, wait, she . . . I was giving her a
massage . . . wait . . . Wait! She came in here . . . she (*to*

CLAIRE) . . . with respect . . . she took off her clothes,
and she got in *bed*, I told her I could not – we don't know
each other, you see . . .

CLAIRE: . . . we had a script conference . . .

JOE: I told her Thank You Very Much, but it was
inconvenient because . . . uh . . . because . . .

ANN: You can do it.

JOE: Because I'd met someone else.

ANN (*very simply*): Oh *okay*.

JOE: You believe that?

ANN: I do if you do.

Pause.

JOE: But it's absurd.

ANN: So is our electoral process. But we still vote.

JOE: Do you truly believe the electoral process is absurd?

ANN: I used to go out with a politician.

JOE: You used to go out with him, you broke up with him?

ANN: Sure did.

JOE: Why?

ANN: Time for a change. Keep your margins straight.

JOE: Yes.

ANN: Go you Huskies!

INT. HALL. NIGHT.

ANN *puts down the typewriter and types into it, 'The truth may
not always set you free, but it is always the truth' – Joseph Turner
White, 'Anguish'. She affixes the lure to it and leaves them on the
typewriter. She starts down the hall, humming. Behind her we see
the door to Bob Barrenger's room open.* BOB *comes out, looks
down the hall. The coast is clear.* CARLA *comes out. They kiss
chastely, say goodnight. She starts down the hall, humming.*

EXT. MAYOR'S PORCH. DAY.

The POSTMAN *walks up. We see two workmen putting up a sign over the door, '1835.' One has a copy of the* Hollywood Reporter *in his back pocket.*

MAYOR: And don't you *worry* about that permit . . .

MARTY: Why, that's right fine . . .

POSTMAN: Mornin' George.

MAYOR: Hey Chunky. (*to* MARTY) Well, we're glad to have you here. My wife . . . Sherry . . . SHER, YOUR BROTHER'S HERE! (*to* MARTY) We're having a *party*, matofact, Tuesday night, for Walt and Bob Barrenger . . .

MARTY: *Mmm* . . .

MAYOR: Havin' 'em over, homecooked meal, if you'd . . .

MARTY: Well, I'd be awfully . . .

A paint truck pulls up outside the mayor's house. Painters come out. SHERRY *comes outside the house.*

SHERRY: Where the hell have you been . . . ? It's . . .

MAYOR: Sherry, this . . .

POSTMAN: (*come back out of house with cup of coffee*) Mornin' Sherry.

SHERRY: It's a quarter after nine, I've been on the phone to . . .

PAINTER: Morning, Mrs Bailey, Mista Bailey . . .

The PAINTER *and his* ASSISTANT *go into the house with wallpaper.*

SHERRY: I've got two days to get this house . . .

MAYOR: Dear, this is Mr Rossen, he is the producer . . .

SHERRY: I am so glad to meet you. We are so glad to *have*

61

you here, and *welcome* you to our . . . I, you know, they
had c . . . I'm, *yearly* I redecorate our, to restore it to the
1835 . . .

MARTY: What is that . . . ?

SHERRY: . . . the house, the 1835. The original *kitchen*, of
course, burned in 1960, as part of a spate of fires . . .

MARTY: It's lovely.

SHERRY: A spate of suspicious fires which were in fact the
inspiration for the formation of the Waterford
Huskies . . .

MARTY: My oh my.

SHERRY: I'm . . . Tuesday evening we're having an informal
dinner, I didn't know you'd be 'on set', but if you'd like
to join your . . .

DOUG *comes up the walk. A bit rabid.*

DOUG: I have to talk to you.

MAYOR: Doug, this is Mr . . .

SHERRY: Oh, how *thoughtless* of me. Would you like a cup of
tea . . .

SHERRY *disappears into the house.*

MAYOR: . . . he's the producer of the movie.

DOUG (*to* MARTY): I want you to hear this, pal . . . (*consults
notebook*) Forget the overages, *forget* Ten Thousand
Dollars for three days to two weeks. You know what it
would cost for them to *build* this set? (*pause*) Two
Million Dollars! Now –

MAYOR: Doug . . .

DOUG: Now: the Waterford Merchants' Association, of who I
am Council . . .

In the background we see SHERRY *and the* PAINTER.

SHERRY: Don't tell *me* you're out of wallpaper.

PAINTER: I told you, we could have it by Wednesday . . .

SHERRY: Wednesday, don't tell *me* Wednesday, the biggest grossing box office star in the world is coming for dinner *Tuesday* . . .

PAINTER : Waal, if you ordered something common . . .

SHERRY: Something common? I'm going to give *you* something common, I'm going to give you an injunction, is what I . . . Mister Mayor . . .

DOUG: Huh. Well, the Waterford Merchants' Association *demands*, through me as their council, five percent of the profits of the movie, as figured by and . . . (*checks his notebook*) geared to the most favorable definition of profits of either A) the *Producer* . . .

From inside the house, we hear SHERRY *screaming. The* MAYOR *runs inside the house,* DOUG *and* MARTY *follow.*

DOUG: Why, you little *sheeny* . . .

INT. COFFEE CORNER. DAY.
Geezers are at the front table in the window. Carla's father JACK *is behind the counter trying to assemble an espresso machine, reading from the instructions.*

MORRIS: 'Assembly of Death' did 95 million dollars the first weekend.

SPUD: Yeaup, but those grosses are inflated.

MORRIS: You think so?

SPUD: Waal, what was the per-screen average . . . ?

JOE *enters and exchanges greetings with the locals. He changes his glasses and takes out a notebook. He is shaking his head as he does so.*

JOE: Cuppa coffee, and a . . .
JACK: With you inna moment. I'm a little shorthanded . . .
MORRIS: Where's Carla . . . ?

ANN *enters.*

SPUD: Hiya, Annie . . .

A crowd has gathered around the table as he tells the story.

MORRIS: Annie, sorry I ain't been to a meetin of the Drama
 club . . .

ANN *shows a swiped 'cancelled' poster of her play.*

MORRIS: Oh, good . . . (*He resumes talking to his companion.*)
ANN: Good morning to *you* . . . whatsa matter?
JOE: I can't get it to come out right.
ANN: What's the scene . . .
JOE: It used to be the Old Mill.
ANN: What've you got?
JOE: They meet on Main Street. Her horse has just died. He's
 coming from the fire.

JOE *shuffles through his pages. He goes in his pocket for a note, he brings out the old lure.*
He smiles at ANN, *she smiles back.*

JACK (*offscreen*): Annie, you want something to eat . . . ?
ANN: What's the scene *about* . . . ?

64

JOE: It's good to see you, *too* . . .

JACK: Annie?

ANN: What about . . . what about . . . it's so presumptuous of me, to be, to be telling *you* how to wr . . .

JOE: *Please* . . .

ANN: How about, he sees her on the street, he wipes the soot from his eyes. He goes up to her. 'What happened to the horse?' She looks at him. She takes his hand . . .

ANN *takes* JOE's *hand, and he winces.*

JOE: Ah. Ah. Ah . . .

ANN: I hurt you?

MORRIS: What happened to his finger?

ANN: It was burnt.

MORRIS: Mmm.

ANN: And then it was *really* hurt.

JOE: Ah. Ah. Ah. That's what she *says,* that's what she *says.* He says, 'Sister, I've come from a *fire* . . . ' But she, but she, she says it was not the fire which hurt you . . . it . . .

MORRIS: . . . how was it hurt?

ANN: . . . he stuck a fishhook in it.

MORRIS *nods.*

JOE: She *realizes* – it was not the fire which *hurt* him . . . that the *true* hurt was her. Was her . . .

ANN: . . . yes.

JOE: . . . her unbridled sexuality. That he . . .

ANN: . . . yes.

JOE: Has been wounded by *her* heat . . . by her *infidelities* . . .

JACK: Anybody here seen Carla?

JOE: Because, because, because if its about *purity* . . . it's . . . it's . . . and then, then, you don't need the *nude* scene.

ANN: Because it's about *purity* . . .

JOE: That's . . . that's *exactly* what it's about. Take . . .

ANN: That's right . . .

JOE: . . . take *any* two people . . .

JACK: . . . anybody seen my daughter . . . ?

JOE: . . . take you and me . . .

JOE *runs out.*

INT. PRODUCTION OFFICE. DAY.

UBERTO *looking at storyboards and spinning the discus and shaking his head.* WALT *on the phone.*

FIRST ASSISTANT DIRECTOR *shows up.*

WALT (*on phone*): . . . the finest people you could ever hope
   to work with . . . (*to* FIRST ASSISTANT DIRECTOR) You
   have the new Old Mill pages?

FIRST A D: I can't find the writer.

WALT (*on phone*): . . . totally false . . . *totally* false. He is the, I
   would say the most responsible human being I have
   ever . . .

FIRST A D: I have to talk to you. My wife . . .

WALT: Not now.

FIRST A D: My wife is going to have a baby, and . . .

WALT: Oh, that's *great.* Let's bring more people into this
   overcrowded world.

GIRL PRODUCTION ASSISTANT *walks through the BG in 'Does
it have to be an old mill . . . ?' t-shirt.*

WALT: Take it off. Take that stupid fucking shirt off right
   now. (*into phone*) Well, if I had to say one thing, I would
   say it's *purity.*

CLAIRE *shows up, dressed in travelling clothes, her luggage behind her, followed by* PRODUCTION ASSISTANT.

WALT (*to* PRODUCTION ASSISTANT): Not now, I'm talking to the press. Claire!

CLAIRE: What? I have a five o'clock plane to catch.

WALT: I, uh . . . (*into phone*) I've always thought so . . . (*beat*) Well, you just get an idea, and try to find the best way to express it in pictorial form. (*to* CLAIRE) I've written a letter to the studio and to SAG protesting – (*opens door*) Bill: get a copy of that letter . . . ! (*closes door*) I just wanted to tell you that I am *past* chagrined, I'm *mortified* at the way you were spoken to . . .

CLAIRE: I . . .

WALT: An artist of your caliber . . .

CLAIRE: I'm only trying to . . .

WALT: I know what you are, I am *so* sorry that you . . . when I read that script I said there's only one person to play that part.

CLAIRE: The minute I read that script I said . . .

WALT: I know . . .

CLAIRE: . . . she works with *animals*, she . . .

WALT: . . . yes . . .

CLAIRE: . . . she has a *home* . . .

WALT: . . . I know, I'm so . . . because I said: yes, a woman who . . . the . . . the community *respects* her . . . (*beat*) Please don't go. (*pause*) Please don't go. What can I do but beseech you . . . ? Trauma, *toil* . . . when are we free of them . . . ? (*pause*) When . . . ?

CLAIRE: He treated me as if I were a child . . .

WALT: Claire . . . (*pause*) As an interpretive artist to a creative artist . . . (*pause*) Stay with me. (*pause*) I need you. (*pause*) We start to shoot tomorrow and then it belongs to *us*. Stay. (*pause*) Stay. Tonight . . . when (*gestures*

outside) when they've gone. Let's talk. Let's *really* talk.
We could, we'll have *dinner*, we'll . . . a bottle of some
bad red wine, we'll get spaghetti, and we'll . . .
CLAIRE: I'm sorry Walt – it's gone *beyond* that.

CLAIRE *exits*.

WALT (*into phone*): Well, I've enjoyed it, too. Any . . . any . . .
any time . . . (*he hangs up the phone*) What does the
woman want from life . . . ?
MARTY: She wants eight hundred thousand dollars to show
her tits.
WALT: Pay her off.
MARTY: We don't have the money.
WALT: *Find* it.
MARTY: If you do the product placement . . .
WALT: IT'S A COMPUTER COMPANY . . . IT'S A
COMPUTER COMPANY, *BAZOOMER-COM*?
MARTY: 'Bazoomer *dot* com.'
WALT: I CAN'T PUT A COMPUTER IN A MOVIE
SHOT IN 1895 . . . you wanna tell me how I'm gonna
do that?
MARTY: Actually, the art department had some ideas on . . .
WALT: No No No No No, pay her off. Did you hear me?
MARTY (*picks up the phone and dials*): Gimme Howie Gold.
Howie? Thizz . . . I nee . . . I NEED EIGHT
HUNDRED GRAND. I . . . I don't care where it comes
from . . . (*to* WALT) It comes out of our end. (WALT
gestures <u>do</u> it.) I . . . I need . . . JUST GET ME THE
MONEY. I . . . JUST GET ME THE GODDAMN
MONEY . . . Look –

JOE *barges in*.

JOE: She doesn't show her tits!!! She doesn't show her tits.
     The breasts symbolize motherhood, the audience . . .
MARTY: The breasts symbolize motherhood . . .

INT. WALT'S OFFICE. DAY.
JOE *holding forth to* BILL, WALT, *and* MARTY. JOE *consults his notes, changes his glasses, reads on*:

JOE: The movie's about *purity*. So we don't *show* her breasts.
     We show them to *him*, her back to the camera.
WALT: . . . she keeps her back to the camera . . . ?
BILL: It'll hurt the box office.
JOE: They know what her tits look like.
WALT: Know? They could draw them from memory. You're
      fantastic. What a find you are. Get outta here. We need
      the Dead Horse Scene.
JOE: I'm gonna nail it.
WALT: I know you are. Go you Huskies.

JOE *exits. We see the notation, 'Dinner with the Mayor'.*
We see MARTY *walk up to a* PRODUCTION ASSISTANT *in the next room. The* PRODUCTION ASSISTANT *hands* MARTY *a slip of paper.* WALT *goes to them.*

MARTY: We got the permit.
WALT: Is that one hell of a kid?
MARTY: He just saved us eight hundred thousand bucks.
WALT: He's got a gift for fiction.
MARTY: We got to do something nice for *him*.

MARTY *takes out his cardcase.*

MARTY: Gimme a pencil. Get him a bottle of . . . get him

69

some maple syrup. Stick this card on it, and put it in his room.

P A: Maple syrup?

MARTY *writes on the card.*

MARTY: Yeah.

Angle insert: the card. It reads: 'Your gift for fiction makes everything sweet.'
Angle on WALT *as he walks back into the other room, holding the permit.*

MARTY (*in BG as he takes back the card*): Hold on, I wanna *add* to that.

We see him take the card, write 'Over' on it, and draw an arrow.

EXT. MAIN STREET. NIGHT.
JOE, *happy as a clam, sauntering down the street. Smoking a huge cigar. He passes the two old codgers,* MORRIS *and* SPUD.

SPUD: You see where Tom Miller's playin' the Old Farmer?
MORRIS: He's been playin' the Old Farmer nigh on sixty years.
SPUD: I read for that part. Did pretty good too.
MORRIS: Bet you did.
SPUD: But I couldn't r'member all the words. Ast them would they gimme a second chance.
MORRIS: Ain't no second chances in life.
SPUD: Zat true?
MORRIS: Only second chance we git, z'ta make the same mistake twice . . .

Angle on JOE, *as he nods, to himself, takes out a pad, starts to jot a note, fumbles with his glasses.* JOE *saunters on, writing, we hear the beeping from the traffic light.* JOE *hears a screeching of tires. He looks up. A film station wagon comes barreling around the corner, hits the pothole, goes out of control, careens, turns over, knocks down the control box of the traffic light.* JOE *holds a beat, runs over to the car, to driver's side. Battered driver, bleeding, upside down.* JOE *drags him from the car. It is* BOB BARRENGER.

BOB: Get the . . .
JOE: Are you al . . . ?

BOB *points to the other side.* JOE *looks.*
Angle: his POV. CARLA *is the passenger. She is dazed but unhurt.*
Angle: the car.

BOB: We gotta get her out of here . . .

CARLA *has extracted herself from the wreck, stands, woozily, on the sidewalk.*

BOB (*to* CARLA): Are you all right . . . ?
CARLA (*nodding*): I . . .
BOB: You got to get out of here . . .

Beat. CARLA *nods, understanding. A light comes on in the apartment over the store.* CARLA *looks up, starts away down the street. Beat.* BOB *rocks back and forth.*

BOB: Oh God, oh God, oh God . . . do you have a cig . . .

INT. BOB'S HOTEL ROOM. NIGHT.
BOB *is being bandaged by* DOC WILSON. MARTY *on the phone.*

WALT, *the* FIRST ASSISTANT DIRECTOR *and* JOE *also in the room.*

MARTY: He's fine . . . it's a . . .
DOC WILSON: You're going to be fine. I'll stop by tomorrow.
WALT (*to* DOC WILSON): Thank you.
DOC WILSON (*exits*): *Yessir . . .*
MARTY (*into phone*): He's . . . you wanna talk to . . . ?

BOB *goes over to the phone, his head bandaged.* WALT, *smoking, stands by the window.*

BOB (*into phone*): Hello, Jerry. I'm fine. I'll be ready
    Wednes . . . I'm here to make a movie, Jerry. Now don't
    you worry your, hey, pal, when have I ever let you down
    bef . . . Okay, babe, you too.

BOB *hangs up.*

WALT: Are you okay?
BOB: Well, yeah, I'm fine, I reached over to, the girl had to be
    home, I don't know, it's a *schoolnight*, something . . .
WALT: *Bobby* . . .
BOB : Everybody needs a hob . . .
FIRST A D: Walt, I wonder if I could take a minute of your
    time. I need a day off . . .

There is an abrupt knocking at the door.

WALT: Who is it?
CAL: Thiz the Police. Is Mr Barrenger in there . . . ?

The boys in the room go into a whisper conference.

72

MARTY: Okay, look, you, what is she, nineteen, twenty . . . oh
  Christ . . .
BOB : Uh, *look* . . .
MARTY: Look: okay. Okay. Look: look you're driving,
  countryside, so on, you picked her up, she was hitch . . .
WALT: No, hey, hey . . . al, she hid in the back of the car!
  Happens all the . . .

The knock is repeated.

CAL (*outside the door*): Is Mr Barrenger there . . . ?
MARTY: No, wait a, wait a, wait a . . . we can't put her in the
  car, she gets it in her head to sue, or Rape, or some
  goddam, she wasn't in . . .
WALT: She wasn't in . . . you were al . . .
MARTY: There's no witnesses . . .
WALT: No, just the . . . there's no witnesses, right . . . ?
BOB: No, I . . . just . . . just Joe, just Joe . . .
WALT: Joe, the writer?
BOB : Just him and me.

Knocking is repeated.

MARTY: Then she wasn't in the car. *Say* it.
BOB : She wasn't in the . . .
MARTY: Nobody knows it but us. All right? It stays *here* . . .
  (*to group*) Are we together on this? (*beat, each nods*)
  Because it's sink or swim here, pals . . .

They murmur their assent. Knocking is repeated. WALT *goes to
the door.*

MARTY (*to* FIRST ASSISTANT DIRECTOR *and* JOE): You guys
  had better leave us a . . .

73

CAL: Mr Barrenger.

MARTY *ushers* JOE *and the* FIRST ASSISTANT DIRECTOR *out of the room.*

MARTY: Yes . . . ?

CAL *comes into the room.*

CAL: I'm very sorry to . . .
MARTY: Well. What seems to be the . . . ?
CAL: I have, to ask you these . . . um. You have a valid
    driver's licence . . . ?
MARTY: Of course he . . .
CAL: Could I see it please . . . ?

BOB *gestures to his wallet which is on the desk.*

CAL: Were you under the inf . . .
BOB: No.
CAL: And who was driving the . . .
BOB: I was alone in the car. I was driving.

CAL *is writing down these statements.*

CAL: Well, now, Mr Barrenger, I'm very sorry, in fact, I'm as
    sorry as I could be, *but* . . .
MARTY: I'm an attorney, if there's anything you have to say
    to . . .
CAL: . . . I have to give you this *ticket* for damage to city
    property. I'm really sorry, Sir, it's a formality, I hope
    you'll excuse . . .
MARTY (*beat*): You have to what?

CAL *reaches in back of him, on his belt, and takes out not the cuffs, but the summons book, and starts to write a summons.*

CAL: It's a formality. Any case of damage to city prop . . . you hit the control box of the new stop light, and . . . (*apologetically he hands the ticket to* BOB) They'll, uh, these things *happen*, I hope you're all right, and that you're feeling . . .

MARTY: Well, Officer, don't worry ab . . .

CAL: If there's anything I . . .

MARTY *walks him out into the hall. Photographers and onlookers in the hall. Phone rings.* WALT *answers it.*

WALT (*to phone*): Yeah. *Hello*, Mr Mayor . . . Walt Price! No, no, sir, he's fine. Well, he's right here! Would you like to . . . ? (*covering phone, to* BOB) You are not to see that girl again . . . do you . . .

Door to hall opens. CLAIRE *comes in.*

CLAIRE: Hello.

WALT (*to phone*): . . . he's right here, Mr Mayor . . .

CLAIRE (*to* BOB): Bob are you alright . . . ?

EXT. FIREHOUSE & PRINTSHOP. NIGHT.
The firetruck is being backed into the firehouse. Outside a couple of passersby are running in the rain, putting their collars up. We see JOE *is in the firehouse writing in his book. As the firetruck backs up we see the firedog bark, and* JOE *looks up. Angle: his POV.* ANN *is walking past the firehouse.* JOE *comes out to look at her.*

JOE: Hi.

ANN: Hi.

JOE: Where you going?

ANN: Going home.

They start to walk down the street in the rain.

JOE: Going home, yeah. I told them what you said . . .

ANN (*over a clap of thunder*): What?

JOE: I told them what you said about the script . . .

They take refuge under the awning of the printshop.

ANN: I didn't say anything special, I was just talking out loud.

JOE: . . . how *else* can you talk?

ANN: No, that's true.

JOE: No. You, I told them, you can't betray with the picture
    what you're saying with the words. And, I don't know,
    the movies, I don't know. They should be socially
    uplifting, why does she have to show her br . . . what is
    this . . . ?

*They look in the window of the old printshop, the awning under
which they have sheltered.*

ANN: Yessuh. Joseph Knights printshop. Vacant for thirty
    years.

JOE: Is it . . .

ANN: Yep. 'N' it's for sale. (*pause*) One of the few things
    money can buy.

JOE *looks in the window of the printshop.*

ANN: Would you like to *see* it? I've got the key back at my store . . .

JOE: I'd love to.

Angle: ANN *runs out into the rain,* JOE *runs alongside her. In the BG, we see the* FIREMAN *closing the doors of the firehouse, and the firedog being restrained, on a leash, by him, and shut up inside the firehouse.*

EXT. BOOKSHOP. NIGHT.

ANN: How's your scar?

JOE: Gosh, you look nice.

ANN: . . . what . . . ?

There's a huge flash of lighting and a clap of thunder and the lights on the street flicker, and come back on. Beat.

INT. BOOKSHOP. NIGHT.

JOE: What would you do with it, the printshop . . .

ANN: Start back up the *Waterford Sentinel.* Town newspaper. Show you the plans . . .

ANN *goes into the washroom area, and comes out with two towels. She throws one to* JOE, *and begins toweling her hair with the other. She hands him some plans, which show photos of the old printshop, and copies of the old* Waterford Sentinel, *circa 1900.*

JOE: Yes, it's a lovely idea . . .

ANN *emerges from the back room. She has stripped off her wet jacket and shirt, and put on a light stockboy's jacket.*

ANN: Print it right here.

77

There's another clap of thunder, and all the lights go out. Pause.

ANN: Oh, my. (*Pause*) Life in the country. One second.

ANN takes a small match from the drawer, and lights a small kerosene barn lantern.

ANN: Well. *There* you go.

ANN sits down on the couch, and spreads the plan on a small table.

ANN: Press still works.
JOE: It does?
ANN: Did as of last week.

She shows him the poster for 'Trials of the Heart'.

ANN: Best way I know to get ink on your hands.
JOE: You'd do the newspaper right here.
ANN: That's something a man could do . . . ?
JOE: You now what else a man can do?
ANN: What?

He moves closer to her. He is about to kiss her when the firedog appears on the couch between them.

ANN: One moment . . .

ANN goes in the pocket of her jacket, the dog follows her. She cannot find a dog biscuit.
Beat. JOE *pats the dog on the head. Leads him to the front door, puts him out. The door blows in the rain.*

JOE: Pelting down out there.

ANN: People might be better off. They thought about it, spent the evening back in the . . .

ANN comes close to him. The dog reappears between them. JOE looks around, and goes back to a window, and shuts the window. ANN crosses to her desk. Takes out a box of dog biscuits. The box is empty. The two of them lead the dog out, and pet it on the head. They turn back and the door is slammed.

EXT. BOOKSHOP. NIGHT.
Beat. They start back to find the door locked.

ANN: Left the keys inside, in my jacket.

JOE nods.

JOE: Well. S'pose I should be getting home . . . Look.

They turn and CAL, the policeman, is standing next to them. In raingear.

ANN: Cal . . .
CAL: Annie . . . got an umbrella . . . ?
ANN: Nope.
CAL: I'll walk you home, you can have my coat.

CAL starts taking off his slicker.

ANN: Then you'll be wet.
CAL: I'm goin' off-shift. Come on . . . I'll walk you home.

CAL covers ANN with his slicker, and they walk away.

We see in the background UBERTO *and his helper, at the firehouse.* UBERTO *swings a shuffleboard disk, and the dalmatian window shatters and falls in the street. Some falls on his head.*

INT. COFFEE CORNER. DAY.
DOUG *talking to the* POSTMAN.

DOUG: Ten dollars apiece for outdated textbooks you or I
    could buy retail for a dollar ninety-five. . .

CARLA *is serving breakfast, her wrist in a cast and a small bandage on her forehead.*

DOC WILSON: Mornin' Carla . . . how's the itching . . . ?
CARLA: Okay, Doc.
DOUG: Bear with me, now – because what're we getting for
    our money? . . . See the cat and dog . . . ? See what I'm
    saying? Nice to take this opportunity to mount an
    investigation of . . .

CARLA *assembles a tray, starts out the door, as* MAUDE *comes in.*

MAUDE: Morning, Carla, what happened to you . . . ?
DOC WILSON: She went to fetch a pail of water.

CARLA *goes out the door.*

INT. WALT'S OFFICE. DAY.
WALT, MARTY, BOB, CLAIRE, JOE, *coffee urns. They work on the script.*

WALT: So you see what I'm *saying* . . . the movie is about
80

purity . . .

BOB: I've always seen that.

WALT: We *don't* show her breasts, we just show your
     reaction . . .

CLAIRE: I'm so comfortable with that, Walt, I can't *tell*
     you . . .

WALT: Well, Joe said it, and he's right.

Knock at the door. MARTY *goes to the door.*
Angle: CARLA *outside the door, talking to* MARTY. MARTY *takes
tray.*

CARLA: And I have Mr Barrenger's Tuna B . . .

MARTY (*hands her a bill*): Thank you.

CARLA: I, well, you know, I tried to take him, in his room.

MARTY: I think he's moved . . .

CARLA: I, uh . . . (*pause*) Um . . .

Angle: inside the room. MARTY *closing her out.* BOB *and* CLAIRE
talking.

BOB: That makes a *lot* of sense, Claire, that makes a lot of . . .
     list . . . listen, cause the audience isn't *coming* to see your
     breasts. They are coming to see you *act*. What are you
     doing this evening . . . ?

CLAIRE: I'm having dinner with W . . .

WALT: We're going to discuss the scr . . . you wanna come
     along . . . ?

BOB: You mind . . . ?

CLAIRE: No, are you kidding me, Bob, not at all.

WALT: Marty . . .

MARTY: Yeah?

WALT: Would you, tell the guy, get the AD, someone,
     somewhere where we can *get away*, something, I want,

you know, last day before the shooting, get away, forget it, have some local food. (*to* JOE) You want . . .

JOE: I've got a date.

WALT: He's got a date, he's got a date, is this guy fantastic . . . ? Already he learned how to write a movie, and he found a girl to get his toes curled, what a guy, what a . . . what a literary find . . . !

FIRST ASSISTANT DIRECTOR *walks in, talking on a cellphone.*

FIRST A D (*on phone, sotto*): I'm trying, honey . . . I'm . . . look, is your Ma, when is your *Mom* coming? Oh. (*pause*) What did the *midwife* . . . ?

WALT: Did you, where are we going tonight . . . ?

FIRST A D: I . . . ?

WALT: Some, you were, you were going to make a reservation for us? Where's my schedule? Where are we *booked* tonight?

FIRST A D: My *wife's having a baby* . . .

WALT: You what . . . ? Is that on the call sheet, is that on the call sheet, or is that *personal business*? Ah, Christ. *Marty* . . . Are we *paying* you?

FIRST A D: I . . .

EXT. REALTY OFFICE. DAY.
The Real Estate office. The placard with the 'Old Printshop' advertised. The REALTOR *taking the placard out of the window.*

INT. BAR. A.M. DAY.
The BARTENDER *is looking down studying a vast book, 'State Statutes of Vermont'.* DOUG *drinking.*

DOUG: She didn't even finish knitting me the sweater . . .

FIRST ASSISTANT DIRECTOR *walks in.* DOC WILSON *walks in.*

BARTENDER: Mornin', Doc . . .

DOC WILSON: You doin' here, Doug, thought you started out the day with that pernicious *caffeine* . . .

DOUG: Kiss my ass.

DOC WILSON: Well.

BARTENDER: He had a hard day. Ann's deserted him for some guy on the movie.

DOC WILSON: Well, they don't always leave with the ones they came in with.

BARTENDER: Big day last night.

DOC WILSON: Hope to tell you. Didn't I pick the fragments of glass out of Bob Barrenger's actual head myself.

Angle: in the BG we see CARLA *entering with bags of food and checks for bar patrons.*

BARTENDER: Mornin' Carla.

CARLA: Mornin' Uncle Ron.

DOC WILSON: Cluster of events. Don't see something, ten year, allasudden. Three times inna night.

BARTENDER: That's what they call an events cluster. Some guy, nobby orders a Manhattan, fifteen, twenty years, allasudden, three times inna night.

DOUG: Who got their heads cut?

BARTENDER: . . . some fella. Orders a manhattan.

DOC WILSON: What?

DOUG: Who got their heads cut?

DOC WILSON: Uh. Bob Barrenger, fella, *cameraman* . . .

DOUG: You said *three* . . . ?

DOC WILSON: *Did* I? I think you're mistaken.

83

Angle on DOUG, *looking over at* CARLA, *with a small cast on her wrist and her head beneath a babushka, in the lobby.*
DOUG *looks up.*

INT. CORRIDOR TAVERN MOTEL. DAY.
CARLA, *being led by the hand by* DOUG. *Following them, her father* JACK *and* CAL *the trooper.*

CARLA: I wasn't in the car . . .
DOUG: We're going to s . . .
JACK: Doug, she says that she wasn't in the c . . .

They stop at a room, knock on the door. A paunchy SALESMAN *opens the door.*

SALESMAN: Yeah?
DOUG (*beat*): I've got the wrong room.

The procession reverses, starts down the hall, runs into MARTY *coming out of his room.*

DOUG (*to* CAL): Arrest him.
MARTY: What is the . . . ?
DOUG: Arrest him.
CAL: For what . . . ?
DOUG (*beat*): Conspiracy in Statutory Rape.
MARTY: Conspiracy in Statutory Rape. Okay. Of whom?
DOUG: This young woman.
CARLA: Nobody touched me, I was at home.
MARTY (*to* CARLA): Who is it raped you?
CARLA: Nobody.
MARTY: Well, what's the beef?
DOUG: She was in the car with Bob Barrenger last night. And

she was injured coming home from a love tryst, so . . .

MARTY: You were in the car with Bob?

CARLA: No.

MARTY: Then what is the . . . ?

MARTY *steps back into a linen closet, takes* DOUG *with him by the lapels.*

INT. LINEN CLOSET – HOTEL HALLWAY. DAY.

MARTY: Now what is this, you sonofabitch, because if you haven't heard about the laws of Malicious Prosecution, you're about to. DON'T FLINCH WHILE I'M TALKING TO YOU, YOU TWO BIT SPEEDTRAP FRAUD. There's an old saying, two scariest things in the world, a black man with a knife and a Jew with a lawyer. Now, I am a lawyer, and I am *The* Jew, and you continue ONE MOMENT with this slanderous shit here in this public place, I'm going to have your ass over my mantelplace. THE KID WAS NOT IN THE CAR, SHE SAYS THAT SHE WASN'T IN THE CAR, NO ONE SAYS THAT SHE WASN'T IN THE CAR, NO ONE SAYS THAT SHE *WAS* IN THE CAR, YOU HAVE NO CORPUS AND YOU HAVE NO CASE, AND YOU *KNOW* IT. SO I'M NOT PAYING PATSY WITH YOU HERE, YOU MOTHERFUCKER. Look in my eyes: I made eleven million bucks last year and I don't like being trifled with. Now I think that the better part of valor, though we've got your back up, here . . . the better part of valor is to step away. Or, before God, I will see you disbarred. (*beat*) Now, what do you think? (*beat*) We all have a movie to make. Now, can we stay together here . . . (*pause*) What do you say . . . ? Have a cigar.

MARTY *puts a cigar into* DOUG'S *pocket.*

INT. HALL. DAY.
The two come out, MARTY *with his arm around* DOUG.

MARTY: It's a mistake. It's all over. (*to* CARLA) I'm sorry that
    we've inconvenienced you.
CARLA: I wasn't in the car.
MARTY: We know that you weren't.

They walk down the hall. Before them, CLAIRE, *half clothed,*
backing out of a motel room.

CLAIRE . . . because you treat me like a *child* . . . you treat me
    like a *child* . . . *that's* why I can't come . . .

The procession has reached the open door. They look to see whom
it is CLAIRE *is addressing.* CARLA *looks in the door.*
Angle: CARLA'S *POV.* BOB BARRENGER, *clutching a towel to*
his naked self, smoking a cigarette.
Angle: the group in the hall. CARLA *points into the open door.*

CARLA: He took advantage of me.

INT. PRODUCTION OFFICE. DAY.
MARTY, CAL, BOB BARRENGER, WALT, DOUG, CARLA, JACK.

MARTY: . . . upset and impressionable . . . (*to the* FIRST
    ASSISTANT DIRECTOR) Get me the mayor . . .
BOB (*to* CARLA): . . . I was just talking to that girl in the other
    room.
MARTY: . . . overcome by the events around her, the presence

of a high-powered . . .

BOB (*to* CARLA): I never touched her. My mother's gr . . .

MARTY: And a *fantasy* object . . .

DOUG (*to* CAL): Tell him to get dressed . . .

CAL: Uh, sir . . .

The FIRST ASSISTANT DIRECTOR *enters with law books, marked as to page.*

MARTY: (*takes law books*) Wally . . . ?

WALT: Look, Carla. This is a hard time for you. Many young
     people go to Hollywood. I did . . . And we all dream of
     it, and here, here Hollywood has come to you . . .

CAL: Mr Barrenger, I'm very sorry, but . . .

WALT: Here this dream world has come to you. Now, you
     obviously have an active, a vivid imagination.

CARLA: Her . . .

BOB: I swear that that woman in my room . . .

WALT: Be quiet, Bob. A fertile mind. Now we can use that
     kind of people in our work. Yes, we can. Now, and this
     is what occurs to me. There's a part in the film . . . isn't
     that right, Marty . . . ?

MARTY *is perusing the law books.*

MARTY: Mmmm.

WALT: That we could use you in and I think that's quite a
     fine trade-off all around and an ill wind that blows
     somebody good.

MARTY (*of the book*): Here it is: Statutory r . . . Blah Blah,
     Blah, Blah . . . 'statutory' . . . 'Unsupported testimony by
     the . . .' (*he shows the book to* DOUG) Hold on, Bobby . . .
     (*to* DOUG) You've got nothing, and you know it. By
     God, you know it. Harassment. You need a . . . Even if

this was true, you need a witness. You need someone
puts her in the car, and you've got nothing. Now we all
have . . . yes, give her that part in the film. (*to* CARLA)
Yes, we'd love to have you . . . Now: we all have more
important things to do, isn't that right . . . ?

MARTY *starts ushering everyone out of the room.*

MARTY: Isn't that right? I'm sorry that you all went to this . . .
JACK: I *knew* that she wasn't in the car . . .
MARTY: This has been just an unfortunate . . .

MARTY *ushers them out. The phone is ringing.* WALT *picks it up.*

WALT (*into phone*): Yes? Hello, Mr Mayor. Nothing, just an,
an unfortunate . . . (*he covers the phone*) It's the Mayor,
he's saying . . .
MARTY: Is he cool or angry?

INT. MAYOR'S HOUSE – DAY.
MAYOR *on the phone.* SHERRY *in the background.*

MAYOR: Well, these things happen. *Purpose* of my call, my
wife wanted to know what brand of *cigarettes* Mr
Barrenger smokes, so she could lay some out tonight . . .
we got the list of his dietary *requirements* . . .

INT. PRODUCTION OFFICE. DAY.
WALT (*hangs up phone*): So we just got lucky.
BILL: Marty, it's Howie Gold on the coast, he needs your
confirmation on a request for money . . . ?
MARTY: And I need a drink.

MARTY *exits.*

WALT (*to* BOB): If your memory was as long as your dick,
you'd be in good shape. How long since you almost went
to jail for this shit?

BOB: How could she turn on me like that? I thought she liked
me.

WALT: Can we try to keep our pants buttoned and get out of
this town in one piece?

BOB : I'm ready!

MARTY: Stay ready. Stay by yourself in your room.

BOB : What'll I do for fun?

MARTY: Whyn't you learn your lines?

BOB : I *know* my lines . . .

WALT: You do . . . ?

BOB : I just don't know what *order* they come in . . .

WALT *walks away from* BOB, *shaking his head.*
Angle on MARTY *and* WALT *as they walk down the stairs.*

WALT: I tell you what, let's ditch these cockamamie locals. I
need to get outta here. Go to some roadhouse tonight,
just us, Claire, Bob, siddown, have a bottle of wine. Tell
me where we're going, and let's go.

They walk by the bullpen, wherein we see PRODUCTION
ASSISTANTS *refilling Evian bottles from a ratty old watering
can.*
PRODUCTION ASSISTANTS *take us, with their Evian bottles,
into Walt's office, where we see the 'Dinner with the Mayor' sign.*

INT. MAYOR'S HOUSE. NIGHT.
Twelve overdressed people, including the POSTMAN, *the*

SPORTING GOODS STORE OWNER, *etc., sitting, still around the Mayor's laden dining table. Beat.* SHERRY *looks over her shoulder.*
Angle: in the next room, the MAYOR *on the phone. Hushed.*

MAYOR: Well, you must, where did they . . . where . . . I . . .

Pause. Very angry. He hangs up, looks out the window.
Angle: his POV. The MAYOR *lets the shade drop, walks back to the table. Silence. Beat.*

INT. BAR. NIGHT.
DOUG, *in his cups, at the end of the bar with the* FIRST ASSISTANT DIRECTOR.

DOUG: Hey, you've gotta eat a peck of dirt . . .
FIRST A D: My wife just went into labor . . .

The BARTENDER *studies his state statutes book.*
We see his POV. Inside the book the storyboards show the movie's heroes copulating.

DOUG: Half a buck I'd close it down . . . it's per . . . you
    know, it's perfidy, you got your Barrenger, molesting
    little girls . . .
FIRST A D: He should be put in jail.
DOUG: Half a buck I'd put him in jail . . .
FIRST A D: You should.
DOUG: I had a witness I would.
FIRST A D: A witness to what . . . ?
DOUG: You know, to the rape, to . . . even to the accident . . .
FIRST A D: You mean *with* White . . . ?
DOUG: What?

FIRST A D: You mean you need a witness in addition to
    White . . . ?
DOUG: Who's White . . . ?
FIRST A D: The writer.
DOUG: (*beat*) He saw the accident . . . ?
FIRST A D: Sure.
DOUG: He saw the girl in the car . . .
FIRST A D: You bet he did.

INT. MAYOR'S HOUSE. NIGHT.
The MAYOR *and* SHERRY *alone at the table. The* MAID *emptying
trays of food, untouched, into a galvanized steel garbage pail
placed in the middle of the room. One of the guests leaving,
putting on her coat. Dips back into the dining room to try to pick
up a tray of pate.*

SHERRY: Don't you *touch* that . . . I want them gone.
MAYOR: I signed the permit. I don't know how I can.
SHERRY: I want them thrown in jail.
MAYOR: Sherry, Sherry . . .

*She empties it into the trash. Beat. The guest, chagrined, leaves.
The* MAYOR, *sitting drinking booze out of a large glass. The
phone rings. Beat. He goes to it.*

MAYOR (*into phone*): What . . . ? (*he jiggles the receiver*) Get
    me the State Police.

EXT. PRINT SHOP. DAY.
*A sign in the window, 'Sold', is stamped over and reads 'Under
Agreement'.*
Early summer morning. JOE, *holding a cup of coffee, looking at*

91

the print shop. ANN *walks up.*

JOE: Good morning.

ANN: Sleep well?

JOE: Yeah, you?

ANN: Oh yeah.

JOE: I've been thinking: look at this: we live up here . . .

ANN: Yes . . .

JOE: We could live up here, live up in the country.

ANN: Now you're talking . . .

JOE: . . . and we could get up every morning . . .

ANN: . . . well, we do that *anyway* . . .

JOE: And come to the printshop. You know *why* . . . ?

ANN: . . . the better to eat me with, your dear?

JOE: To print the newspaper. And I'd come to *write.* To
write. To write. Right here in the office.

ANN: Not without a rolltop desk.

JOE: Well, I could *get* a rolltop desk.

ANN: Happen to know where there's one for sale.

JOE: Well ain't you amazing.

They walk on, onto the scene of various filmfolk setting up.

EXT. STATE AND MAIN. DAY.

ANN: Lookit that, up already.

JOE: That's why we filmfolk get along so well with you
farmers. Both up with the chickens.

*They push through the mass. The street is closed off by Police
cars.*

They come upon a TV REPORTER, *doing a standup in front of the
firehouse, where we see, in front, both the old firetruck, and state
trooper cars.*

TV REPORTER: . . . where Movie Star, Bob Barrenger, fresh
    from his troubles with the law *last* year . . .

Angle on ANN *and* JOE, *as they look on.*
Angle on a STATE TROOPER *and* DOUG, *as they walk through
the crowd.* MARTY *walks up to the* TV REPORTER.

TV REPORTER: . . . is once again in hot water. Involved in a
    car crash last night with a young, a very young woman,
    Mr Barrenger is being arraigned today for . . .
MARTY: You better make sure you got your facts straight,
    pal, 'cause, you step off the line and I'm going to sue you
    personally for . . .

The TROOPER, DOUG, *and* BOB *walk up to* MARTY.

TROOPER: We're looking for Joseph Turner White . . .
MARTY: Oh, good, yes. Good morning. Where are you taking
    Mr Barrenger?
TROOPER: We are looking for a Mr Joseph Turner
    White . . . ?
MARTY: What are you doing with Mr Barrenger?
DOUG: He's under arrest . . .

DOUG *hands the arrest warrant to* MARTY.

MARTY: Oh, good. I'm his *lawyer* . . . and you must be Perry
    Mason. Guess what, you're about one half step from a
    world of hurt . . . how diverting . . . the Mayor's gonna
    have your ass. Can I watch?

Camera takes the group, the TROOPER, DOUG, BOB *in
handcuffs,* MARTY *talking with them, through the crowd, at the
back of which we see* ANN *and* JOE.

DOUG: Well you guess what. The Mayor sent me. I have
   your Mr Barrenger with a history of . . .
MARTY: . . . a history of *nothing*, he was acquitted . . .
DOUG: Moral turp . . . you're on my home court, friend, I
   have the Mayor and the town behind me, and forget
   making your movie: I may own the studio when I get
   through with you: I got a civil suit, I got rape, I got
   collusion . . .
MARTY: You've got nothing, you don't have a witness . . .
DOUG: And I've got a witness! Your Mr White saw the crime.
MARTY: He told you that . . .
DOUG: He didn't have to tell . . .
MARTY: want to talk to him. Would you ex . . .
DOUG: Oh, you're his attorney, too . . . ?
MARTY: Later for you, pal.
DOUG: Okay . . .

He motions the TROOPER *to take out* BOB. MARTY *sees* JOE *in
the back.*

MARTY: Bobby, don't say anything.
BOB : Nothing happened.
DOUG: We'll see about that at the inquest.

Angle on MARTY *as he leads* JOE *down into an alleyway, and
into a backyard, hung with washing on the lines.*

MARTY: Yeah, hi, pal, I need to talk to you . . .

INT. BOOKSHOP. DAY.
ANN, JOE, *and* MARTY. CAL *has followed them into the
bookstore. He speaks privately with* ANN *and exits.*

94

ANN: What is it all about?

JOE: I saw . . .

MARTY: How do they know that, you told them?

JOE: No.

MARTY: What did you say to them . . . ?

JOE: I didn't say anything to them.

MARTY: How do you know you saw it?

JOE: I don't know.

MARTY: Well, then, you didn't see it, right . . . ?

JOE: I don't . . .

MARTY: You didn't see it . . .

JOE: I . . . ? I saw it. I was there.

MARTY: You were there. At . . . at 10:35 . . . ?

JOE *takes the arrest warrant, looks at it, changes his glasses.*

JOE (*as he reads*): I was walking down the street . . . I
    remember, I was writing a . . .

MARTY: What glasses were you wearing? (*pause*) Were you
    wearing your reading glasses . . . ?

JOE: I . . .

MARTY: You told me you were writing. Don't you wear your
    reading glasses to write . . . ?

MARTY's *cellphone rings and he answers it. After a pause, he
hangs up.*

MARTY: I've got to go to the jail.

MARTY *exits, leaving* WALT *alone with* ANN *and* JOE.

Angle on ANN. *She sees something down the other street. We see*
CAL, *the policeman, enter and start toward* JOE, *we see* ANN
restrain him and speak to him in the BG for several moments.

95

CAL *shakes his head, and* ANN *reasons with him, and there is a pause and he looks at* JOE, *and exits. Beat.*

ANN: . . . he's going to give you a couple of minutes.

Pause. JOE *walks* ANN *off to the <u>closed</u> back door of 'The Waterford Players'.*

JOE: What am I gonna do?
ANN: You got to tell 'em that you saw the accident. Don't you?
JOE: I can't do that. (*pause*) If I tell them, they'll, if I *tell* them, they'll try Bob for Rape, they'll . . . it'll ruin his career . . .

Pause.

ANN: But that's what happened.
JOE: But it'll stop the movie.
ANN: Maybe they'll be *other* movies.
JOE: They'll . . . they'll *blackball* me . . .
ANN: Carla was in the car, right?
JOE: I . . . I *think* that's right . . .
ANN: . . . you think that's right . . .

Pause.

JOE: What'm I going to do . . . ?

ANN *picks up a copy of the old* Waterford Sentinel, *which was left on the coffee table. She hands the paper to* JOE.
Angle: JOE *holds the paper.*
*Angle insert: the masthead reads, '*Waterford Sentinel, *All the News of the Mountains, "You Shall Not Bear False Witness".'*
Angle on ANN, *who has also picked up the 'For Sale' sign,*

showing the printshop. She stands looking at JOE. *Beat.* CAL
enters. They look towards him.

CAL: Lotta hubbub on the street. I'm taking you the back
way.

EXT. BACKYARD OF THE BOOKSHOP. DAY.
CAL *walks with* JOE; *still holding the newspaper. As they round a
house corner,* WALT *appears and walks with* JOE.

WALT (*checks watch*): Let's speak English. You've got to help
the side.
JOE: You want me to lie.
WALT: On the contrary. I want you to tell the truth. (*pause*)
The truth is, you can't tell me, to a certainty, that you
saw the thing. You don't remember, a gun to your head,
which glasses you have on. And you have a fertile
imagination. Imagination wants to fill in the blanks.
Now. If you aren't *sure*, then they have nothing. Bob
walks free. As he should. (*pause*) Joe: wasn't long ago
they buried actors at the crossroads with a stake through
their heart. You know? The people who are talking to
you about the way we live though we may praise them,
we fear them. And they fear us. Because we tell the
truth. About our lives. Now, this is a damn roust, and
everyone knows it; the guy is looking for a case, he wants
to make a name for himself. If we let him do that, if we
let him do that, then we're being false to our community
. . . to our community, you understand . . . ? To our
world. 'Cause you are a part of that world, now. You
have to take off the Steel Rolex and put on the Gold
Rolex. (*pause*) And be part of your world. I got a five
picture deal with the studio. And you stick with me. You

97

write one, two more, you stick with me, and you'll *direct* the third one. You are a part of this world. It's in your blood. It's you. You *have* to do the right thing: we're out in the Provinces, the Sheriff *literally* is at our door. You have to stand with the troops, Joe. That's the bottom line. You *have* to . . . if you had the leisure to think it through, you'd see it for yourself. The girl wasn't in the car.

CAL *takes* JOE *to a side door of the courthouse.*

INT. SMALL COURTROOM. DAY.
JOE *coming in through the side entrance of the courtroom. Various law books and dusty forms on the shelves.* CAL *leads him into the courtroom, empty, save for the* COURT REPORTER, MAUDE *and the* BAILIFF. CAL *motions* JOE *forward.*

CAL: . . . Joseph Turner White . . .
BAILIFF: Hear ye, hear ye. Sixth District Court. And for the county of Kadona, State of Vermont, the honorable James Addison Flynn presiding. All those having business before this court, draw forward and you will be heard.

JUDGE *enters.*

BAILIFF: All rise.
JUDGE: Please . . . Mr White . . . ? This is a simple matter of . . .

The CLERK *hands him a sheet of paper.*

JUDGE: Uh huh . . . all we need's a simple fact or two . . .

You're going to give your recollections of the accident
last evening, at the corner, State and Main. Would you
please swear him in.

BAILIFF: Do you swear to tell the truth –

EXT. MAIN STREET. DAY.
A crowd, moving along, with the TV REPORTER.

TV REPORTER (*talking to camera*): . . . the arraignment, as we
said of Bob Barrenger, *the* Bob Barrenger, star of 'The
Old Mill', about to begin shooting here, in picturesque
and sleepy . . . (*sound of shouting, and reporter looks
around*) we should say, *formerly* sleepy . . . Yes, yes . . .
it's . . . yes, it's Claire *Wellesley* . . . and we're going to
try to get a look at . . .

The crowd moves away, revealing ANN, *standing in front of the
realtors, looking at a card in her hand. She looks up to see* JOE
coming toward her.
Angle: Extreme close up, ANN *smiles.*
Angle: Extreme close up, JOE. *He looks toward* ANN, *sheepishly.*
Angle: ANN, *as she looks down at the card in her hands.*
*Angle, insert: It is the real estate placard for the printshop,
marked 'Under Agreement'.*
Angle on ANN *as she rips it up.*

INT. LOBBY OF THE HOTEL. DAY.
JOE *coming in, a hangdog look on his face.*

PRODUCTION ASSISTANT (*to* JOE): They need those rewrites
on the Old Mill Scene . . .

JOE *nods. Continues through the lobby.*
Angle on various reporters, CLERK *being interviewed.*

CLERK: . . . about his personal life . . . though I *can* tell you a
   few things about . . .

JOE *walks past.*

JOE: Would you please hold all calls to my room?
CLERK: Though I can tell you a few things about his dietary
   requirements.

The old BELLHOP *is packing up his lunchbox and changing into
his street clothes.*

INT. JOE'S ROOM. DAY.
JOE *enters and takes out his pad and pencil. He sits on the bed.
On the pillow, he sees and picks up a black and red hunting jacket
on to which the short sleeve has been knitted in baby blue wool.
There is a card in the pocket that reads 'Better than new – it's got
a story!' He puts it down.*
JOE *picks up his notebook, in which he has written: 'The Purpose
of the Second Chance is to allow you to make the same mistake
twice.'*
JOE *stops by the mirror on the chiffonier into which he puts the
lure, which still has the attached card reading 'The truth may not
always set you free, but it is always the truth' – Joseph Turner
White, 'Anguish'.*
JOE *goes to the bed. On the bed is a small package tied with
ribbon.* JOE *opens it.*
*Angle insert: It is a small thing of maple syrup. Attached to it is a
card reading: 'Your gift for fiction makes everything sweet.'*
JOE *takes off his jacket, and picks up his notebook. Out of his*
100

jacket pocket falls the old copy of the Waterford Sentinel. *He picks it up.*
Angle, his POV. The masthead: 'Waterford Sentinel, All the News of the Mountains, "You Shall Not Bear False Witness".'
JOE *puts the newspaper down. Picks up the maple sugar card again, and looks at it. He sees an arrow, and turns it over.*
Angle insert: The back of the card reads: 'How about an Associate Producer credit . . . ?'
JOE *takes the paper, balls it up and throws it into the trash. He picks up the fishing lure which is resting on the typewriter. Puts it into his pocket, thinks again, throws it in the trash. Shakes his head, and picks up his suitcase and starts packing.*

EXT. ANN'S STREET. DAY.
On DOC WILSON, *as he walks down the street. A little kid* (BILLY), *on a scooter, is going in the other direction.*

BILLY: Mornin', Doc . . .
DOC WILSON: Mornin', Billy, where ya goin' in such a hurry?
BILLY: Down the corner, see the ruckus . . .
DOC WILSON: Watch the *curbs*, now . . .

Angle on JOE, *as he stands across from Ann's house looking at it. He holds his suitcase.*

DOC WILSON (*of his suitcase*): Where you off to?
JOE: I, uh . . . I'm leaving.
DOC WILSON: Why?
JOE: I perjured myself. (*Pause*) I told a lie, and I ruined my life. That's what I did . . . (*shrugs*) I don't suppose you could help me with *that*, could you? Turn back the *clock*, or something? Give me back my, give me back my *purity*, I don't suppose you could just wave your magic

wand and do that, could you . . . ? But what *is* truth? Eh?
Int that the thing? What *is* true?

DOC WILSON: It's the truth that you should never trust
anybody, wears a bowtie. Cravat's s'posed to point down
to accentuate the *genitals*, why'd you wanna trust somebody, s'tie points out to accentuate his *ears* . . . ?

JOE *turns, to see* DOC WILSON *swigging from his flask. In the BG
we see the* BELLHOP *walking. Beat.*

JOE: Aren't you supposed to set an example for people . . . ?

DOC WILSON: Nope. I'm just supposed to hold people's hands,
while they die. What'd you say your problem was . . .

JOE: . . . I just swore my life away, back in that . . .

DOC WILSON (*as he sees an older woman off on a porch to the
side*): Mornin, Chessy . . . how's the back . . . ?

DOC *walks off to his office.* JOE *walks away, toward the station.*
BELLHOP *walks through.*

EXT. RAILROAD STATION. DAY.

JOE: I ruined my life. Isn't that funny, that you can actually
do it in one moment just like they say. I ruined my life
back in that courthouse.

BELLHOP *has walked up beside him.*

BELLHOP: What courthouse?

JOE: Courthouse back in town.

BELLHOP: Town ain't got no courthouse.

JOE: What?

BELLHOP: Ain't got no courthouse. Courthouse burnt down,
1960.

The train is arriving. The STATIONMASTER *puts out the steps to help the people down.*

JOE: Well, where do they hold court?
BELLHOP: Hold court, they have to, science lab, the high
    school.

An elderly-looking JUDGE *fellow descends from the train, follow by a* CADDY *with his golf bag.*

STATIONMASTER: Mornin', Judge, what brings you here?
JUDGE: I'm s'posed to hear some deposition, some fool, saw
    the accident last night.
JOE: . . . the courthouse burnt *down* . . . ?
STATIONMASTER: Yep. Courthouse burnt down, 1960. Part
    of a spate of fires, Old Mill, Courthouse. S'posed to've
    been set by some deranged teenager.

JOE *looks around.*
Angle, his POV. The old BELLHOP *walking down the tracks.*
Angle on JOE, *as he turns back into town.*
Angle c.u. on the STATIONMASTER

STATIONMASTER: Yep, never did discover who set 'em . . .
He smiles, and lights his cigar.

EXT. COURT HOUSE BUILDING. DAY.
We see the crowd has moved down the street and the 'Courthouse' building is empty.

INT. 'COURTHOUSE'. DAY.
JOE *enters, and the camera takes him into the deserted building,*

103

through the courtroom, and, in back, he sees ANN *standing alone.*
He walks back to her, through the doors which appear to be the
Judge's chambers.
Angle, reversed. We see that the walls of the Courtroom are a set,
and we are back in the 'Trials of the Heart' set. ANN *is sitting*
there. Reading her play by Joseph Turner White . . . He looks at
her for an explanation. MAUDE, *the 'court reporter' woman, is*
sitting in the background. ANN *is knitting in pink wool.*

ANN: I thought you needed to get it out of your system.

ANN *moves to embrace* JOE. *They hear screaming. They turn.*

EXT. MAIN STREET. DAY.
Angle, their POV. At the end of the alleyway, in Main Street.
We see SHERRY, *the Mayor's wife, leading a crowd.*

SHERRY: . . . A blight, a blight and an obscenity . . . that's
    good English, isn't it? How's that for entertainment . . . ?

Angle: the mouth of the alleyway, on Main Street.
Angle insert: the baseball on which is written 'To Chuckie! From
your pal, Bob Barrenger.'
Angle: the distorted face of Chuckie, heaving the baseball.
Angle on BOB BARRENGER *being led through the crowd, a*
baseball hitting him in the back of the head, as troopers hustle him
toward the courthouse. In the BG ANN *and* JOE *emerging in the*
alleyway.
Angle on ANN *and* JOE.
JOE *starts to cross the street. We see the airport van.*

ANN: What are you going to do?
JOE: I'm going to tell the truth.

104

They cross the street. In the background a little man with a bag (HOWIE) *gets out of the airport van.* JOE *and* ANN *walk toward the crowd at the mouth end of the high school.*

INT. HIGH SCHOOL CORRIDOR. DAY.
A crowd of people, TV technicians, and a view of DOUG *on a TV monitor.*

DOUG: . . . and to exterminate this vermin, yes, I use that
    term, who have abused, who have *desecrated*, yes, the
    license granted to them by a gracious nation.

Angle on MARTY *and* WALT, *standing near the monitor, looking on. Shaking their heads.*
Angle on the monitor. DOUG, *seen through the monitor.*

DOUG: . . . who spew filth and degradation . . . (*he begins*
    wiping his head. As he does so, a makeup person comes in
    and sponges him.) . . . thank you . . .
TV REPORTER: . . . you want to clean up . . . ?

Angle on DOUG, *seen 'live' in the next room, starting to wipe his brow.*

DOUG: Yes, thank you.
Angle: MARTY *and* WALT *watch* DOUG, *as he walks down the hall.*

TECHNICIAN: Five minutes, and we're going live to the
    network.
DOUG (*to himself*): . . . foreign, and unamerican *perversions* of
    the Democratic process. By those we have entrusted
    with our dreams . . .

Angle on MARTY *and* WALT, *looking on.*

WALT: Do something.
MARTY: You tell me what to do, I'll do it.

They look on to the preparations for the TV.

WALT: . . . and I was just paying off my house in Malibu . . .

ANN *and* JOE *push through the crowd.*

WALT: Thank God, it's up to you, Pal. 'S'up to you . . .
JOE: I'm out.
WALT: I don't getcha.
JOE: The girl was in the car.
WALT: I treated you like a son or nephew.
JOE: It's not *you*, it's . . .
WALT: No, what is it?
JOE: I have to tell the truth.
WALT: . . . that's just so *narrow* . . .
JOE: The girl was in the car.
WALT: Then you're finished in show business.
JOE: So be it.
WALT: And my company sues your ass for sixty million
    dollars.
JOE: For what cause?
WALT: I don't need a cause, just a lawyer.

HOWIE GOLD *shows up holding his bag.*

HOWIE: *I'm* a lawyer . . .
MARTY: Howie.
HOWIE: Yeah?
MARTY: What are you doing here?

106

HOWIE: What am I doing here is I just flew seven hours cause
    you asked me here.

WALT: What for?

HOWIE (*presenting the bag*): For this . . . I hope you need it,
    cause it's coming outta your budget . . .

Angle insert: The bag as MARTY *opens it. It is full of money.*

INT. HIGH SCHOOL LAVATORY. DAY.
DOUG *is mopping his face up. He looks up.* MARTY *is standing
there.*

MARTY: Hi.

DOUG: I'd prefer it if you didn't speak to me.

MARTY: I . . .

DOUG: . . . you know, there's nothing you could say, that
    could *possibly* make a difference, so, why don't you just
    save your breath.

MARTY *puts the case up on the washstand.*

DOUG: What's in the case?

MARTY: Eight hundred thousand dollars in cash.

Pause.

DOUG: And what was it you wanted to say?

MARTY: Gut Yuntif.

INT. HIGH SCHOOL CORRIDOR. DAY.
ANN *and* JOE *passing through. They stop and* JOE *comes up to a*
STATE TROOPER.

JOE: I'm supposed to give my deposition . . . ?
COP: We'll *be* with you in a minute.
ANN: I'll wait for you . . . I'm proud of you. I'll be waiting.
JOE: If I go to jail . . . ?
ANN: I'll knit you a sweater.

The TROOPER *nods, and begins to lead* JOE *through the mob. As we press forward the mob begins to reverse direction and passes back towards* JOE. *Leaving the Hall empty, save for the* JUDGE *who comes out, putting his robe into his golf bag.*

JOE (*to* JUDGE): I've come to give myself up.
JUDGE: Well give yourself up to someone else. I'm gonna get in some *golf.* Hiya, Annie. Give yourself up to her.

And we see JOE *has moved up to the TV monitor, where we see* DOUG, *in the science lab, talking to the press, and holding his money bag in his arms.*

DOUG: I have learned a lesson. And the lesson is *this* . . . that everybody needs a second chance. You, me, and these fine film people here. You know, they have a high profile, but that doesn't mean they aren't deserving of our trust, and of our respect. You know, I think there is a lesson here, and the lesson is this: it is a lesson of *Tolerance* . . . and, as we look at this industry, at this clean, *American* industry, and as I begin my campaign for Congress . . .

Dissolve.

EXT. MAIN STREET. DAY.
WALT *on the scene, talking with the* CINEMATOGRAPHER *and*

108

the CAMERA OPERATOR. *Preparing the first shot.* The FIRST
ASSISTANT DIRECTOR *instructing the extras.*

FIRST A D: Okay. Are we getting set up here . . . are we
getting set up . . . *People* . . . ? Can we *settle* . . . can we
settle now . . . ?

EXT. REALTY OFFICE. DAY.
The placard marked 'printshop' comes back out of the window.

EXT. MAIN STREET. DAY.
Angle on ANN *as she, holding the placard, starts to cross the
street. An* OLD FARMER *smoking a pipe, driving a pickup is
stopped by a* PRODUCTION ASSISTANT *talking on a walkie-
talkie. We see that it is the 'Judge' who listened to Joe's
testimony.* ANN *waves to him, and proceeds to the Old Firehouse,
where they are about to make a movie.*

FIRST A D: Okay, this is a *picture* . . .

ANN *stops at the back of the crowd of onlookers. She waves to
someone.*
Angle: her POV. It is JOE, *sitting near the director, who waves
back.*
Angle on ANN, *who is next to* CAL, *the policeman, now in leather
jacket and leaning on his Harley motorcycle.*

FIRST A D: Quiet please . . .

Angle. The slate reads 'The Fires of Home'.

EXT. MAIN STREET – THE FIREHOUSE. DAY.

Where they are filming the characters in turn of the century garb.
BOB BARRENGER, *dressed as a fireman, is polishing the old fire*
engine. The actor playing DOC MORTON *walks past.*

DOC MORTON: Mornin Harry. Heard you had a little fire last
    night . . .
FIREMAN: Waal, you didn't have nothin' to do, Doc,
    wouldn't life be *dull* . . . ?

Two NUNS *walk by.*

BOB: Mornin', sister.
CLAIRE (*dressed as a* NUN): We missed you in Church today,
    Frank.
BOB: Sister, I've just come from a *fire* . . .

Angle on JOE *sitting near the camera, looking through the script.*
Reading along, mouthing the words. He wears the plaid jacket.
One sleeve is blue, knitted.
Angle: The onlookers. ANN, CAL *next to her lounging on his*
motorcycle. GRACE *and* MAUDE, SPUD *and* MORRIS, *the*
POSTMAN, *the fake* JUDGE, *who is also the man smoking the pipe*
in the first sequence and is smoking a pipe now, the CLERK *from*
the hotel, et cetera.
Angle showing the crew, and the film within the film. We see the
livery stable across the way. On its side are painted various ads.
Among them one which says: 'Stefan P. Bazoomercom' and
MARTY *is standing next to it. Looking on at the scene being*
filmed. An ASSISTANT DIRECTOR *brings him a cup of coffee.*
The FIRST ASSISTANT DIRECTOR *passing out pink bubblegum*
cigars, the bands of which read 'It's A Girl!'
Angle showing the film within the film, and the group at the
camera watching transfixed.

110

NUN: . . . to come by *next* Sunday, and we'll give you a
    second chance.

BOB: Only second chance I know, chance t'make the same
    mistake twice.

NUN: Well . . . time will tell.

She walks past the 'Bazoomercom' ad.

FIRST A D (*holding cellphone to his ear*): That's a cut . . . !

Angle on ANN *and* CAL*., as they talk the firedog comes over and*
ANN *gives him a dog biscuit. In the BG we see the man with the*
pipe get into his pickup and drive off. The POSTMAN *goes off*
continuing his rounds.
Angle on ANN *and* CAL *as they talk. Next to them* MORRIS *and*
SPUD *congratulate each other. Next to them we see the fake*
JUDGE *and the* BAILIFF.

CAL: Mom's expecting you for dinner tonight.

ANN: I'll be there.

CAL: You bringing your new friend?

ANN: Sure plan to.

CAL: (*pause*) He have any special dietary requirements . . . ?

ANN: He'll eat potroast and like it.

CAL: Go you Huskies?

ANN: You bet your life.

Angle on JOE*, as he looks over at* ANN *and smiles.*
Angle on ANN*, giving him a 'thumbs up' sign as the firedog comes*
and sits next to her. In the BG, we see the pickup hit the pothole
and bounce.
Fade out.

Works of David Mamet available from Methuen

ISBN	Title	Price
0 413 57450 4	American Buffalo	£6.99
0 413 69370 8	The Cryptogram	£6.99
0 413 55420 1	Glengarry Glen Ross	£6.99
0 413 73570 2	The Old Neighbourhood	£6.99
0 413 62620 2	Oleanna	£6.99
0 413 19280 6	Speed-the-Plow	£6.99
0 413 64590 8	Mamet Plays: 1	£9.99
0 413 68740 6	Mamet Plays: 2	£9.99
0 413 68750 3	Mamet Plays: 3	£9.99

* All Methuen books can be ordered online at www.methuen.co.uk. They are also available through mail order or from your local bookshop.

Please send cheque/eurocheque/postal order (sterling only) Access, Visa, Mastercard, Diners Card, Switch or Amex.

Expiry Date: .... Signature: ....

UK customers please allow £1 for the first book and 50p thereafter up to a maximum of £3 for post and packing.
Overseas customers please allow £1.50 for the first book and 75p thereafter up to a maximum of £5 for post and packing.

ALL ORDERS TO:
Methuen Books, Books by Post, TBS Limited, The Book Service, Colchester Road, Frating Green, Colchester, Essex CO7 7DW.

NAME ....

ADDRESS ....

....

....

Please allow 28 days for delivery. Please tick box if you do not wish to receive any additional information

Prices and availability subject to change without notice.